"All of us hurt when we are rejected. But for some, this experience is so crushing that it is not clear how to ever bounce back. In this well-written and carefully crafted book, Leslie Becker-Phelps invites readers on a psychological and social journey in which rejection and fear of rejection are allowed to shine a light on how we relate to our own experience. All of it—including our sensations, thoughts, emotions, actions, and the mentalization of ourselves and others. By learning to take a self-compassionate approach to experience, the reader is shown in a step-by-step way how to turn rejection into greater attachment and connection—with others and with your deeper self."

—**Steven C. Hayes, PhD**, Foundation Professor in the department of psychology at the University of Nevada, Reno; codeveloper of acceptance and commitment therapy (ACT); and author of *A Liberated Mind*

"This book is very helpful for those who have recently been rejected or who would just like to have healthier relationships with others. Grounded in solid psychological theory and research, it unpacks why we get stuck in old patterns and how to get unstuck. Highly recommended."

—**Kristin Neff, PhD**, associate professor in the department of educational psychology at The University of Texas at Austin

"This book gets right to the heart of overcoming rejection sensitivity—compassionate self-awareness. Using exercises that are easy to apply in daily life, Becker-Phelps offers a positive pathway to feeling more safe and secure in our relationships. She also unpacks in accessible prose the important connections between attachment theory and self-compassion practice. Highly recommended!"

—**Christopher Germer, PhD**, Harvard Medical School/ Cambridge Health Alliance; author of *The Mindful Path to Self-Compassion*; and coauthor of *The Mindful Self-Compassion Workbook*

D1236908

"*Bouncing Back from Rejection* is a wonderful primer for anyone who is struggling with rejection and is curious about gently attending to these sensitivities. By tapping into our basic human needs for love and belonging, Becker-Phelps offers practical and compassionate ways to redirect attention away from chronic self-criticism and toward cultivating a deep sense of self-worth, security, and self-kindness—ultimately fostering resilience for the quirky challenges of being part of the human family."

> —**Tara Cousineau, PhD**, staff psychologist at Harvard
> University Counseling Center; senior faculty at the Center for
> Mindfulness and Compassion, Cambridge Health Alliance,
> Cambridge, MA; and author of *The Kindness Cure*

"This book first reveals the immense power that fear of rejection can have over us. Then, clearly and compassionately, Leslie Becker-Phelps shares the puzzle pieces—awareness, reflection, and reframing—that can release our fear and create a newfound sense of freedom."

> —**Sharon Salzberg**, cofounder of the Insight Meditation
> Society, and author of *Real Happiness* and *Lovingkindness*

"For anyone struggling with actual or perceived rejection by others, this book provides a lifeline. Leslie Becker-Phelps clearly understands the issue, including its anticipation and painful aftereffects. She offers a variety of very practical strategies for making changes based on an integration of contemporary treatment and self-help approaches. A book that compassionately and comprehensively attends to a topic that gets far too little attention."

> —**Christine A. Courtois, PhD, ABPP**, licensed psychologist in
> private practice (now retired); consultant and trainer in
> trauma psychology and trauma treatment; coauthor of
> *Treating Complex Trauma*, with Julian Ford; and author of
> *Healing the Incest Wound*

"*Bouncing Back from Rejection* will help you uncover the courage, self-worth, and resilience that are naturally at the foundation of who you are. Take your time with it, absorb it into your life, and watch the gifts grow."

—**Elisha Goldstein, PhD**, founder of the Mindful Living Collective, and creator of A Course in Mindful Living

"In *Bouncing Back from Rejection*, the generous and passionate author gives us all she has, drawing on the science of attachment, mindfulness, and compassion-focused imagery. Feelings of rejection are at the heart of so much of our emotional suffering. What better path, than a path to self-acceptance, inner security, and kindness?"

—**Dennis Tirch, PhD**, founder of The Center for Compassion Focused Therapy, associate clinical professor at Mount Sinai, and author of *The ACT Practitioner's Guide to the Science of Compassion*

BOUNCING BACK *from* REJECTION

**BUILD THE RESILIENCE
YOU NEED TO GET BACK UP
WHEN LIFE KNOCKS YOU DOWN**

LESLIE BECKER-PHELPS, PhD

New Harbinger Publications, Inc.

Publisher's Note

Distributed in Canada by Raincoast Books

Copyright © 2019 by Leslie Becker-Phelps
           New Harbinger Publications, Inc.
           5674 Shattuck Avenue
           Oakland, CA 94609
           www.newharbinger.com

Cover design by Amy Shoup

Acquired by Jennye Garibaldi

Edited by Karen Levy

Library of Congress Cataloging-in-Publication Data on file

Printed in the United States of America

21   20   19

10   9   8   7   6   5   4   3   2   1   First Printing

Contents

Foreword

Why do we need a book about moving from rejection to resilience? It's because we humans didn't evolve to be happy. Instead, our brains evolved to help us survive and reproduce. Activities that contribute to surviving and reproducing—like eating, keeping warm, and having sex—instinctively feel good. Experiences that threaten our survival—such as being injured, thirsty, too cold, or too hot—feel bad. Any of our ancestors who didn't share these reactions, who weren't hard-wired to act in ways that supported survival and reproduction, didn't get to pass their DNA on to us.

In prehistory, one of the greatest threats to our survival was rejection. Imagine our ancestors, living in groups of 25 to 50, roaming from place to place on the African savanna one hundred thousand years ago. They needed one another to hunt for food, for protection from hostile animals, and for mutual care when someone fell ill or was injured. To be rejected from the tribe was a death sentence—no one lasted long alone on the savanna.

Any of our ancestors whose brains hadn't evolved to dislike rejection would have alienated others, been thrown out of the tribe, and died without heirs. So we didn't inherit their DNA. Instead, we inherited the genes of ancient hominids who survived by worrying a lot about being accepted and included.

Even in modern times, being accepted matters a lot. We humans are born completely dependent on adults. As infants, we can't eat, keep warm, or protect ourselves from injury without adult care. One of our very first survival tasks after taking our first breath is to find a way to connect safely to adults who will care for us. To this day, having a brain that is hungry for acceptance and fearful of rejection is essential for our survival.

But while our instinct to avoid rejection has had enormous survival value, it sure causes a lot of unnecessary suffering. When someone we know passes us on the street or in a hallway and doesn't say "hello," what happens in our heart and mind? When a friend doesn't call or we find out about a party to which we weren't invited, how do we feel? When our colleague gets the promotion and we don't, what goes through our mind?

While sometimes we're able to consider that our acquaintance was preoccupied, that there wasn't room to invite everyone to the party, or that our colleague deserved the advance more, most of the time we also feel disappointment—or worse. We may go into a tailspin, wonder what we did to alienate the other person, muse about why we're not part of the in-crowd, or feel inadequate about our skills. We can easily suffer a self-esteem crash that makes it hard to see our situation objectively and may lead us into a cycle of withdrawal or avoidance that robs us of opportunities to fully engage in our lives.

What to do? Fortunately, we humans didn't only evolve instincts to hate rejection. We also developed ways to manage these feelings and cultivate antidotes—ways to grow from our emotional injuries, separate our fears from real dangers, gain perspective on our strengths and weaknesses, soothe ourselves when injured, and safely connect to others.

In the pages ahead, you'll find a practical, step-by-step guide that anyone can use to harness these resilient capacities and turn our hard-wired aversion to rejection into an opportunity to grow and thrive. Seamlessly integrating modern psychological science, ancient wisdom traditions, and years of clinical practice, Dr. Becker-Phelps offers us easy-to-use tools to turn the pain and fear of rejection into an opportunity to live a richer and more rewarding life—giving us a pathway to the happiness that our brains, narrowly focused on survival, don't always provide. While moving from rejection to resilience can at times be challenging, it's a journey well worth taking.

—Ronald D. Siegel, PsyD

Assistant Professor of Psychology, Harvard Medical School

Author of *The Mindfulness Solution: Everyday Practices for Everyday Problems*

Acknowledgments

Writing *Bouncing Back from Rejection* has come at an especially challenging time for me, transforming this project into a life lesson. It has taught me—or more accurately, reinforced and imprinted in my heart—that my life journey is at once wholly mine and a shared venture. I am blessed with many thoughtful and caring friends (including family members). I thank you all for giving of yourselves when I was most in need. This seems a fitting lesson to learn while writing a book about the importance of finding inner strength along with trust in the "emotional availability" of others.

Of everyone who has supported me directly and indirectly in writing this book, I am especially appreciative of my husband, Mark Phelps. He was always ready to encourage me as I trudged along, writing this book and doing my best to get through the other trials of each day. I am also grateful to him for freely offering his considerable editorial support from the first word through to the last sentence.

Finally, I thank, and am indebted to, the editors at New Harbinger, especially Jennye Garibaldi, Clancy Drake, Gretchen Hakanson, and Marisa Solís, for their guidance in helping craft the book that you now read.

Introduction

There are few things you can say with certainty about all people, but this is one of them: every person—both alive and dead—has experienced rejection. And *everyone* has experienced the pain that goes with feeling overlooked, dismissed, or abandoned. The rejection can be from family, friends, acquaintances, and even strangers on social media whom we will never meet. Yet some people are particularly sensitive to it. They feel rejected when others don't intend it, experience small slights as much deeper injuries, and have difficulty moving on from real or perceived rejections.

If you are rejection sensitive, you may respond to feeling rebuffed or abandoned by sinking into despondency, grasping for validation, or lashing out in anger. Rather than viewing the situation as a painful experience to be moved past—or better yet, an opportunity for growth—you might assess *yourself* to be a problem. You might sense that there is something inherently wrong with you that invites rejection, even if you are angry at times with others for rejecting you. You might also believe that you lack the fortitude to overcome rejection. Whatever your inner struggles, they can lead you to feel disheartened, or even hopeless.

These sorts of mind-sets can often lead to a cycle of ups and downs that seems like an unending closed loop, always with the same sinking ending. But there are definitely ways to break the cycle and escape the emotional roller coaster.

UNDERSTANDING THE ORIGINS OF REJECTION SENSITIVITY

Because you are far from alone (despite how you probably feel), theorists and researchers have had an abundance of research subjects and many years to consider and investigate what makes some people more sensitive to rejection, while others are more resilient. One very well-supported

explanation is attachment theory. Chapter 1 of this book offers a fundamental understanding of it and the part it may play in your rejection sensitivity. Then this insight is used to inform the guidance offered throughout
the rest of the book, helping you build resilience.

To give you a general sense of how attachment theory relates to rejection sensitivity, consider this brief overview. The theory, developed by the
British psychiatrist, psychologist, and psychoanalyst John Bowlby, pro-
poses that infants are prewired to form attachments with "older, wiser"
people as a way to enable them to survive. About 60 percent of the time,
these relationships nurture in them an emotionally healthy and strong
foundation. The children feel secure in themselves and in their relationships, and so they are described as having a *secure attachment style*.

However, other children develop an *insecure attachment style*. They
become adults who continue to have some struggles in how they relate to
themselves and others. Experiencing sensitivity to rejection is frequently
part of these struggles. This leaves them to either try desperately to please
others, turn away from emotional ties in an effort to make rejection a
nonissue, or both. All of these responses create obstacles to effectively
coping with rejection and to fully moving forward in their lives.

Although it can seem trite to say that close relationships give life
meaning, there is a lot of truth in it. The sense of connection is often, by
itself, fulfilling. People also frequently feel better about themselves when
they enjoy the company of others who view them positively. In addition,
they usually enjoy life's happy moments—and endure life's painful times—
more when they have supportive friends. But, as you know only too well,
close relationships can also lead to painful feelings of rejection. In learning to free yourself from sensitivity to this, you will discover a more positive view of yourself, along with feeling more secure in close, loving
relationships.

HOW COMPASSIONATE SELF-AWARENESS
CAN SET YOU FREE

Bouncing Back from Rejection guides you toward a more positive relationship with yourself and other people in your life, which can help develop

resilience to rejection. It does this largely by offering the perspective and tools for you to nurture *compassionate self-awareness*—a combination of self-awareness and self-compassion. Self-awareness is explored in depth through five domains of what I call STEAM: Sensations, Thoughts, Emotions, Actions, and Mentalizing. Importantly, nurturing a compassionate response to your own struggles requires self-awareness, as well as self-acceptance and self-kindness. By applying this set of skills to your relationships, you will be better able to successfully resolve rejection-related issues.

While this inner work is important, it does "take two to tango." Your struggles involve interactions with other people and are affected by your understanding of their responses to you. Though this is addressed throughout the book, *Bouncing Back from Rejection*'s closing chapter offers specific guidance on improving and honing your relationship skills to strengthen your connections. As you grow in this area, you will begin to receive more positive responses, and you will be better able to take them in. Together, the inner sense of having value, and the outer validation that you *are valued*, will enable you to feel good about yourself—even when you are sometimes misunderstood, disrespected, dismissed, or devalued by people who may be important to you.

As with so much else in life, this journey is inevitably filled with setbacks, obstacles, and apparent detours. As a result, freeing yourself from rejection can be complicated and seem like an unsolvable puzzle. But it's not. It just takes some direction, effort, and persistence. This book provides you with the first ingredient, though you must provide the other two.

IMPORTANT INSTRUCTIONS FOR READING THIS BOOK

To get the most you can from *Bouncing Back from Rejection*, read it slowly. Take the time to absorb information and consider how it applies to your life. As you complete its many exercises, repeat any that show promise of helping more with repetition. If you struggle too much with an exercise, move on to a different one—perhaps returning to it later.

Although I have organized the chapters and sections in the order that I think would typically be most helpful, feel free to work on the exercises in any order you wish—unless instructed otherwise in a given section.

You will be directed to complete certain exercises before or after others. I also offer suggestions for what to do when you have difficulty with an exercise. As you grow and change, you may find some exercises that were previously helpful take on new meaning, and others that did not seem to do much for you become more helpful.

To help you succeed in freeing yourself from sensitivity to rejection, I recommend that you:

- Dedicate a journal to making notes and completing the exercises in the book. Following this suggestion can be particularly helpful. While you could use independent sheets of paper, this won't have the benefit of keeping your work together where you can easily find previous notes and review them at any point—even returning to them much later. You might want to use a tablet or laptop, though you may find that the physical act of handwriting helps you connect with or process your experiences more fully.

- Begin your personal excursion with the first two chapters, "Feeling Rejected Can Be Complicated" and "Commitment to Change: Concepts and Tools," which offer a foundation for understanding your rejection sensitivity and tools for empowering you to continue working on becoming more resilient, even when the process gets difficult.

- Each day, choose to practice—and re-practice—exercises in this book.

- Occasionally make note of any and all progress in your journal. Sometimes, in looking at the changes they still want to make, people lose sight of those they've already made. So, journaling about your progress can help you maintain perspective and motivate you to keep working toward your goal.

- Keep sticky notes on hand. As you are reading, you may want to skip to another part of the book, or you may be directed to do so.

You can use these notes as reminders of the section that you want to return to.

- Try to accept setbacks as the inevitable events that they are, and use them to practice reminding yourself that you are only human, that you deserve empathy and compassion just like everyone else. (*Learning this is a process that the book, as a whole, addresses.*)

- If you think you need a break from this work (*and it is work*), you might want to give yourself a "vacation." But first, set a date for when you want to consider returning to it. Then enter a reminder on your phone or paper calendar, or write it on your hand, if that's what works for you. At the appointed time, think about whether or not you are ready to reengage.

Your overall goal is to learn and accept in your heart that you have value. Although rejection can hurt—and be deeply painful—it does not mean your true value is any less. As you absorb this, you will also learn to accept rejection as a human experience that you can survive, and possibly even use to help you grow. If you are someone who has suffered emotional trauma or is so deeply plagued by fears of rejection, self-doubt, or self-loathing that it seriously affects your life, I strongly suggest that you also seek the help of a professional therapist to support you in working through this book.

In more than twenty years of private practice, I have treated many people who struggle with this issue, and what I've learned while helping them can help you. In *Bouncing Back from Rejection*, I have consolidated many of the individual dynamics I have seen into various composite characters to illustrate different points. Though I do not revisit most of the characters, I do follow the stories of two of them—Janine and Chad—throughout the book. None of these characters are actual people, but their experiences are very real, indeed, and will probably be familiar to you.

Here's a brief introduction to our "main characters."

At twenty-seven years old, Janine has several good friends and lives in a spacious condo adjacent to a park, where she enjoys going for walks. Although she looks "together" on the outside, she often feels undone on the inside. Janine frequently repeats to herself, practically as a mantra, *I hope they aren't mad at me.* She constantly worries that she will do the wrong thing or people will see that she is incompetent. So, she works hard to be a nice person, going out of her way to help friends and neighbors and trying to ensure that they will like her. But even among her friends, she often fears that they are critical of her or that she is letting them down.

Chad remembers that Linda literally took his breath away when they first met.

She is so amazing, he kept thinking in wondrous disbelief. Although Chad was committed to advancing at his challenging job as a data scientist, his previous fears of disappointing his boss suddenly didn't seem all that important. Head over heels in love, he was euphoric. But unlike fairy tales, his "happily ever after" did not last. In short order, his fears of rejection took hold. *Who are you meeting up with* he would ask Linda, trying to sound nonchalant. But the truth was that he was possessed by jealous thoughts and preoccupied with fears of her leaving him.

Whatever difficulties you have with rejection, they are founded in experiences we all have to some extent. We want to feel worthy and acceptable, and we want to avoid feeling rebuffed. But none of us escapes rejection—whether it is the devastating experience of being dumped by a fiancé on your wedding day or the relatively minor setback of someone not laughing at your jokes. Self-awareness, self-acceptance, and self-compassion are all key factors in helping people cope. I hope that *Bouncing Back from Rejection* helps you embrace these truths and finally transition from being held captive by rejection to breaking free and embracing life.

CHAPTER 1

Feeling Rejection Can Be Complicated

It's just too hard, young Chad thought, struggling with his homework. As a third grader, he already saw himself as "stupid." It would be another year before his parents had him tested and discovered his language-processing disorder. Like his two older brothers, he would continue to do well in school, but unlike them, he would have to work extra hard. He always persisted in school assignments because he feared losing his teachers' approval if he didn't do well. Out on the playground, he happily played catch, which he was good at, but he kept quiet. *Smile*, he'd remind himself when he didn't understand jokes the other kids were telling, or why they were laughing. *Just throw the ball*, he would tell himself to get his mind off the fear that they would laugh at him if they knew how dumb he was.

Not all rejection is equal. It might be tough for you when your friend balks at your suggestion to go to Poopies restaurant for dinner. (Yes, it is a real restaurant.) Or, you may be in shock as your spouse announces out of nowhere that your marriage is over. Or, you may be facing anything in between. So, your reaction to rejection will obviously depend on the situation. But if your reactions tend to cause further problems—such as creating constant self-doubt—then you would be wise to change them. Life will continue to deliver the challenging situations, great and small, that have caused you to struggle with rejection. But adjusting the way you respond to those challenges is something you can learn.

DYSFUNCTIONAL REACTIONS TO REJECTION

When you are sensitive to rejection and experience it as particularly threatening or extremely upsetting, there are a number of ways that it can throw you off track. See if any of these reactions to rejection, along with the examples I provide, feel familiar to you.

Overreacting

When people chronically brace themselves against a potential threat, they often react quickly to situations—even before they know that they really are in danger. This general dynamic causes rejection-sensitive people to see themselves as being rejected even when that is not the case. For instance, Mandy would often overreact when someone was unable to meet her for dinner. She was not able to see that it wasn't because they didn't value her, but because of a simple conflict in their schedule. Another way to overreact is to perceive small rejections as Major Rejections. This would be the case if you reacted to a normally very responsive friend not returning your call one time with a similar intensity as you would to a friend saying she does not like you as a person.

Being Unable to Move Forward

Some people find that they ruminate about rejection. For example, twenty years after graduating from college, Elizabeth still stewed over the roommate who said she no longer wanted to live with her. Meanwhile, across town, Bonnie continues to feel like her husband does not really love her because, before they were married, he had a brief relationship with someone else when the two of them split up for a year.

Responding with Intense Anger

People often respond with fear and anger to being dismissed or ignored, especially by someone they care about. As noted psychologist Paul Ekman stated in his book *Emotions Revealed: Recognizing Faces and Feelings to Improve Communication and Emotional life* (2003, 127–128),

"Anger controls, anger punishes, and anger retaliates." When you are sensitive to rejection, these reactions are frequently magnified. This makes the situation even worse, as Ekman explains: "One of the most dangerous features of anger is that anger calls forth anger, and the cycle can rapidly escalate. It takes a near-saintly character not to respond angrily to another person's anger, especially when that person's anger seems unjustified and self-righteous."

Guarding Against Judgment

Rejection—or the prospect of it—might feel devastating. Many people who are highly rejection sensitive also frequently struggle with feeling unworthy or unlovable. Given those beliefs, it is understandable that they would feel vulnerable and sad. It's also common for them to guard against exposing themselves to rejection by withdrawing socially, constantly presenting themselves in a positive light, or trying to endear themselves to others by being extremely kind and caring. These actions can leave you feeling very alone and as if people wouldn't like you "if they knew the real me."

Responding with an "It Doesn't Bother Me" Attitude

Some people appear as though they don't feel distressed by rejection, but they are actually just trying to distance themselves from their pain by ignoring it. Andrew would buffer himself from hurt by numbing his emotions. It's not that he didn't feel distressed by rejection, but he would distance himself from that reaction. The problem with this is that he really was still upset below the surface. There was one day at work, for example, when Andrew wasn't thinking about anything in particular, yet felt kind of restless. After he snapped at a coworker for asking a simple question, it occurred to him that he was still upset from the night before. Some of his friends posted online that they were at one of their favorite bars, but they had not contacted him.

Being Independent and Self-Sufficient

Some highly self-sufficient people tend not to look to others for comfort, support, or encouragement. Because they avoid exposing themselves to feeling rejected by others, they may not seem to struggle with rejection. However, this can be more complicated than it seems. While Albert had some of these traits and truly enjoyed investing himself in his work, he was also aware of a desire to connect with others and a sense that something was missing from his life by being so self-reliant. Although he did not feel lonely or exactly fearful of rejection, he was uncomfortable when he was not busily working and would have wanted to feel closer to someone—especially his girlfriend, Sharon. But he wasn't sure how to do that, and he also feared that she would be critical of him, not supportive, if he tried to rely on her.

One way to understand rejection sensitivity is to imagine that your skin has been burned. Even a gentle touch can be extremely painful. You would probably be very protective of your burn, not wanting anyone even near it. If someone did touch it, you might respond with fear and anger. And if you lived with this sensitivity for a very long time, you might understandably feel depressed, anxious, or possibly try to emotionally numb yourself to the ongoing pain. In your real life, it is your "self"—you might even say your soul—that is in pain.

YOUR REJECTION SENSITIVITY HAS DEEP ROOTS

As noted in the introduction, these struggles with rejection can be understood through *attachment theory*, which was developed by John Bowlby (1907–1990). After some preliminary work, he first laid out the theory in his 1969 book, *Attachment and Loss*. It is now well established with a proliferation of research over many decades. Here's an overview.

Attachment theory basically says that the way people relate to themselves and others is rooted in their biology and their early life experiences. Infants are born into the world "wired" for connection, or as this theory labels it, attachment. They look to caregivers for their survival needs and for emotional connection. The adults they turn to for security, comfort, and encouragement are called *attachment figures*. (Importantly, people continue to have attachment figures into adulthood, such as mentors, close friends, and spouses.)

With the understanding that a parent's influence has its limits (we'll talk about this in a little bit), let's examine the basics of the parent-child relationship as they relate to attachment. Children learn that turning to their caregivers generally leads to certain responses, such as being comforted and helped, causing anxiety or anger in their caregivers, being ignored, or some combination of these responses. Children's reactions to these responses are the foundation of their *attachment style* (or way of connecting), which they generally carry throughout their lives—though attachment styles are also influenced by life experiences. For example, consider Janine, one of our two recurring characters. Her mother was frequently critical, which left its mark on Janine in the form of chronic feelings of inadequacy within herself and a fear of rejection from others.

Researchers Bartholomew and Horowitz (1991) found support for the idea that people's attachment styles are basically a combination of the way they relate to themselves and to others. They explored these two fundamental elements, which they labeled *model of self* and *model of others*. (These elements combine to create four basic attachment styles, which we will discuss later in this chapter.)

Model of Self

A person's model of self is the way that they think about and relate to themselves. Infants' sense of themselves depends upon how their caregivers (or attachment figures) respond to them, especially in the early years. When caregivers are attuned to the infant's distress and able to calmly and lovingly soothe them, the infant begins developing the sense that they are not just cared for in the moment, but worthy of love. This can then be reinforced throughout their childhood, and, in fact, for the rest for their lives. The positive self-perception enables them to feel calm, as opposed to anxious.

People who hold a model of self that judges themselves harshly have a more *anxious attachment style*. They tend to experience themselves as inadequate, flawed, unlovable, or in some other similar negative way. This model of self leads them to feel great anxiety in relationship to themselves. When you relate in this way to yourself, it is easy to understand why you would expect to be rejected and on the lookout for it. In other words, having a negative sense of yourself naturally leads to a sensitivity to rejection.

Model of Others

A person's model of others is the way that they perceive the emotional availability of attachment figures, people they would turn to during times of distress. When children experience a parent's typical reaction to their distress as being accepted, loved, and comforted, they learn that they can turn to significant others during difficult times. Children who grow up getting no response, or fearing the responses of their caregivers, tend to learn to turn away from those relationships.

They develop a model that perceives others as emotionally unavailable, resulting in an *avoidant attachment style*. They experience others as uncaring, as too weak or flawed to be helpful, or as hostile toward them. Not surprisingly, any or all of these perceptions of others create in them such sensitivity to the possibility of rejection that they avoid emotional closeness. So, even when they have outwardly close relationships, there are thick "walls" that prevent much vulnerability or openness. The lack of emotional intimacy is often not a conscious problem, but can become one. This is especially true when people face overwhelming issues or somehow begin to be bothered by a sense of something important missing in their life.

ASSESSING YOUR MODEL OF SELF

It is important to understand that the model of self is a dimension, or range. Everyone has good and bad days, but different people can generally feel a greater or lesser sense of being lovable and calm, or unlovable and anxious. If you tend to experience yourself in the latter way, you have a more anxious attachment style.

Read over the contrasting perceptions in Figure 1.1 that people can have of themselves. In your journal, or on a piece of paper, copy the scales in that figure (also available online at www.drbecker-phelps.com/home/ bouncing-back/ or http://www.newharbinger.com/44024). Then place a checkmark on the lines to show where in these ranges, on a day-to-day general basis, your perceptions of yourself fall. (We're not looking for a number here.)

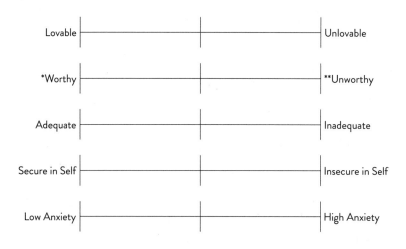

(Anxious Attachment Style)

* Worthy: sound, strong, acceptable
** Unworthy: flawed, inferior, weak, unacceptable

Figure 1.1 Assessing Your Model of Self

Is Your Model of Self Making You Anxious?

Consider the following ways in which a negative self-relationship is often expressed.

Write down each one in your journal (or just on a piece of paper) that you believe applies to you.

Within Yourself

- Feeling insecure, dependent, weak, inferior, flawed, or inadequate

- Feeling not as good or as competent as other people in your life

- Feeling alone in the world (even when others are around or supportive)

- Being self-critical (which can also be self-bullying)

- Feeling shame, self-loathing

- Being angry with yourself for your perceived flaws

- Withdrawing into yourself in response to feeling so negatively about yourself

- Fearful of being overwhelmed by your emotions (believe intense emotions show that there is something wrong with you)

Self in Relation to Others

- Being quick to see others as rejecting you

- Feeling fearful of rejection or abandonment

- Withdrawing from others to avoid rejection

- Being angry with others for not being as available or supportive as you feel you need, or for not somehow making you feel better

- Trying desperately to prove to others that you are worthy

- Being needy or clingy

Reflect on each copied phrase. The more you endorse these phrases, the more anxiously attached you probably are. The phrases you relate to indicate areas that you would benefit from improving. Journal any thoughts you have related to these self-perceptions.

As you work to create a more positive self-relationship, you will notice that you endorse fewer of the above statements and feel less intensely about the ones you do endorse.

ASSESSING YOUR MODEL OF OTHERS

Just as with the model of self, the model of others is a dimension or range of experiences. People can feel others' emotional availability as greater or lesser, leading them to engage more—or less—in emotionally intimate relationships. If you generally experience others as emotionally unavailable, you likely avoid deep emotional connections and do not turn to them as attachment figures who could be comforting. This indicates that you likely have an avoidant attachment style.

In your journal, or on a piece of paper, copy the scales in Figure 1.2 (also available online at www.drbecker-phelps.com/home/bouncing-back/ or http://www.newharbinger.com/44024). Place a checkmark on those lines to show where in these ranges, on a day-to-day general basis, your perceptions of others and your reactions to them fall.

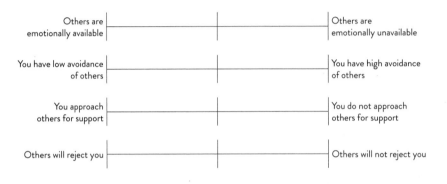

(Avoidant Attachment Styles)

Figure 1.2   Assessing Your Model of Others

Is Your Model of Others Making You Avoidant?

Consider the following ways in which avoiding closeness with others is often expressed.

Write down each one in your journal (or just on a piece of paper) that you believe applies to you.

Self in Relation to Others

- Independent
- Self-sufficient
- Disinterested in their personal matters

Your Perception of Others

- Unreliable or incompetent

- Unsupportive

- Uncaring

- Untrustworthy

- Rejecting

- Critical

- Not available or supportive to others in general

Reflect on each copied phrase. The more you endorse the statements above, the more likely you will feel you are on your own. The more you think of others as failing to be emotionally available *for anyone*, the more likely you tend toward being avoidantly attached. With little to no hope of gaining their support, you are more likely to work hard at being self-sufficient. Journal about these observations.

In reflecting on your model of others, you might realize that you think of others as generally being emotionally available—but not to you. This often happens when people have a model of *self* that leaves them feeling like they are flawed. In this case, you might feel driven to prove your worth to earn others' caring and support. If you relate to this, reflect on and make notes about your inner struggle.

As you learn to see others as emotionally available (to the degree that they truly are), you will feel more connected with them. Relationships will become a personal resource that can support your sense of well-being.

UNDERSTANDING THE FOUR ATTACHMENT STYLES

While two broad styles of attachment—anxious attachment and avoidant attachment—are described above, there are actually four basic styles: secure, preoccupied, dismissing, and fearful avoidant. The first is classified as *secure*, while the other three are classified as *insecure*. These styles can be understood by considering the model of self and the model of others together, as shown in see Figure 1.3 (also available online at www .drbecker-phelps.com/home/bouncing-back or http://www.newharbinger .com/44024).

Figure 1.3 Four-Group Model of Attachment Styles in Adulthood. Based on Bartholomew and Horowitz (1991), Griffin and Bartholomew (1994), and Mikulincer and Shaver (2007).

Secure: People with this style of attachment generally feel good about themselves as people, believing that they are capable, lovable, and worthy of self-compassion when they struggle, even as they face their own weaknesses, mistakes, and flaws. They also see significant others in their life as attachment figures, whom they can rely on as sources of support and encouragement. While rejection (or the possibility of it) is not pleasant, they are able to keep these concerns in perspective and know that they have the resources to cope with it.

Preoccupied (Insecure): People with this anxious style of attachment feel there is something unacceptable about them. They might describe it as feeling unlovable, flawed, or inadequate, and they tend to be self-critical. Although they see others as possible sources of support, they sense that they aren't worthy. So, they often try (and are *preoccupied* with trying) to "earn" the attention or love they need by "performing" in some way, such as taking care of other people's needs or achieving great success in certain areas. However, they sense that it is their performance, not really them, that is getting the attention, support, or love. This leaves them almost constantly distressed by feeling they are still coming up short and in danger of being dismissed, abandoned, or rejected.

Dismissing (Insecure): People with this avoidant style of attachment manage distress by avoiding it. They perceive others as emotionally unavailable, so they don't view them as emotionally valuable—and might even sense that relying on others can be hurtful or disappointing. As a result, they tend to avoid close relationships. At the same time, they also tend to cope with their emotions (which could be overwhelming) by avoiding them. Instead of feeling worthy as a person, they view themselves as having value based on their achievements and ability to manage situations. This style *dismisses* the value of others and of their own inner experiences.

Although their avoidance of emotional closeness makes them less sensitive to personal rejection by others, they are very sensitive to any failure (or potential failure), which they often judge by unrealistically high standards. After all, if they can meet that level of accomplishment, then they must possess value. So they often struggle greatly with self-rejection and self-criticism.

In addition, while those with a dismissing style are not particularly sensitive to rejection by others, experiencing such rejection can trigger an inner rejection. To outsiders, their response to their inner rejection can sometimes look like them doubling down, driving toward higher levels of achievement. In other cases, people with this attachment style might share the self-criticism that drives them, or they might focus more on their previous accomplishments.

Fearful Avoidant (Insecure): People with this anxious *and* avoidant style of attachment sense that they cannot rely on others *or* themselves to feel valued or to calm their distress. These are people who likely experienced their parents as intensely inconsistent—as both scary (based on angry reactions) and scared (based on anxious reactions). So, their attempts to turn to themselves and to others for reassurance are both ineffective. As a result, they are easily upset and their relationships are often tumultuous. Any rejection—real or perceived—can send them spinning into seemingly ever-increasing distress with no clear means of feeling comforted or regaining a sense of feeling valued.

As you think about these attachment styles and which one you best relate to, keep in mind that the categories do not represent four distinctly different styles. Rather, the models of self and others are based on a range of experiences. You can sense that you are more or less lovable and that others are more or less emotionally available. So, if you have a preoccupied attachment style, that label just offers a general description. Your specific style will depend on where you fall along the models of self and others. In addition, your style can change over time with different experiences, and it is often somewhat different in different relationships.

You can gauge where your attachment style falls by considering how well you relate to each of the styles. You might also want to more formally determine your style by taking an online survey (including an empirically validated "Experiences in Close Relationships—Revised" questionnaire) developed by researcher Chris Fraley (Fraley et al. 2011). You can find a link on my website at http://drbecker-phelps.com/home/bouncing-back.

Before placing too much blame on parents for their children's insecure attachment styles, it is important to understand that there can be profound influences beyond any parent's control. Some parents cannot be sufficiently available to their children due to unavoidable circumstances, such as personal struggles with anxiety or depression or perhaps a debilitating illness. Environmental factors, such as being raised in a violent neighborhood or being victimized by peer bullying, can negatively affect a child in ways that are extremely difficult (if not impossible) for a parent to mitigate. Other specific circumstances, such as being adopted, can also affect attachment. Finally, just as no two snowflakes are the same, no two infants are identical either. (I know a bit about this because I have identical twin sons.) Infants are born with different temperaments, such as their reactivity to the environment, mood, and ability to be focused and persistent. Some children have neurological impairments that affect their ability to connect, such as those with autism. All of these factors can greatly affect a child's developing attachment style.

Special note: Throughout this section, I have referenced the importance of feeling accepted and cared about for who you are because you have inherent value. If you believe that what people do is what gives them value, you may not really understand or believe what I am trying to say. If that's the case, then read the "Learning the Truth: You are Worthy and Adequate" section of chapter 8, "Building Self-Acceptance."

HOW YOUR ATTACHMENT STYLE HELPS YOU COPE WITH REJECTION (OR NOT)

While rejection can be painful for everyone, securely attached people do tend to cope with it better than others. These resilient people generally have a positive model of self, and so they feel good about themselves. They also tend to have a model of others as being emotionally available and supportive. So, when they do feel rejected, they can rely on both internal and external support to help them maintain a balanced perspective about it. For example, consider Emily's story:

> Emily always seemed to be able to roll with life's ups and downs. It wasn't that she never got upset or exhibited distress, but when bad things happened, she was able to recover her composure without a great deal of difficulty. As a child, Emily was fortunate to have parents who were not only calm and secure, but who were also able to soothe her when she was afraid, sad, or frustrated. The comfort they supplied gave Emily the solid base to handle life's challenges with confidence and strength.

The following three factors help securely attached people be more resilient to rejection:

Positive Model of Self as Lovable

- By beginning with a sense of being worthwhile and worthy of being loved, securely attached people are able to maintain or quickly regain a positive view of themselves.

- Their self-acceptance supports them in being aware of, acknowledging, accepting, tolerating, and effectively managing their emotions.

- They are more likely to be compassionately self-aware, which can help heal painful emotions.

Positive Model of Others as Emotionally Available

- People who are securely attached generally feel that others are emotionally available to them and value them. So, when they feel rejected by someone or a situation, they can see and feel the true acceptance of others. This broader context keeps the rejection from being devastating, though it can still feel painful.

- With a general openness to others, they are able to consider (and have empathy for) other people's experiences. Reflecting on what may be motivating someone to end a relationship or give critical feedback limits its power. For instance, a securely attached person might be able to recognize that a friend's recent harsh comments stem from exhaustion and stress related to current work problems. While they might view the comments as unacceptable, they can also take them less personally and be less critical of their friend for the transgression. By responding relatively calmly (even if not happily), they can manage the situation effectively.

Positive Model of Coping with Rejection

- People who are securely attached are less likely to make mountains from molehills. Because they have inner and outer resources to help them cope with their feelings of rejection, they are less likely to emotionally overreact or stay in an emotionally reactive mind-set. For instance, rather than turning their partner's plea for them to pick up after themselves into an indictment about them as a whole person or as proof of their partner being a neat freak, they empathize with their partner's frustration about the situation and feel a true desire to lessen it.

- Because they feel positively about themselves and generally cared about by others, they are more likely to be able to risk rejection. So, if they have a problem with how someone treats them, they can feel freer to express their feelings.

- They can deal with a given situation, let go, and move on.

While many people—like Emily—naturally develop a secure attachment style during childhood, not everyone has enjoyed such good fortune. However, attachment styles can be changed. As you read this book and work to create a model of self as more worthy and lovable and a model of others as more emotionally available, your relationship with rejection will begin to change. You won't feel as strong a need to avoid it. Rather than being overly emotional in response to rejection, you will be able to cope better with it, and maybe even see it as an opportunity to grow.

CHAPTER 2

Commitment to Change: Concepts and Tools

Why hasn't Melissa called me back? Janine thinks. It's been a couple of weeks since she and her friend went to the movies, and she can't figure out what she did wrong to make Melissa not want to talk with her. Putting her hand to her chest, she can feel her heart racing almost as quickly as her thoughts. *I really need to get a grip. I can't let my anxiety overwhelm me again.* With that thought, she decides to take a couple of deep breaths. Knowing that writing in her journal often helps, she sits down and scribbles out her thoughts and feelings. Reflecting on what she wrote, she thinks, *My fears about Melissa are getting out of control. I mean, it's not like we always talk every week.* Next, she decides to take a shower and then go run some errands. By that afternoon, she isn't exactly cured of her fear that she somehow offended Melissa, but she isn't overly worried about it, either. She decides to journal more later, focusing on her thoughts, emotions, and what she can do to deal with this situation.

With some effort, you can transform yourself into someone who is more resilient to rejection. As with any worthy endeavor, the path will include obstacles and setbacks. It will also involve having to face rejection and practice responding differently to it, which can feel as enticing as putting your head in a lion's mouth. However, learning more about the process of change, and about how you can help yourself through it, will make it less daunting as it equips you to do the work. So that's what this chapter is about.

Here you'll learn how to approach change with openness and sensitivity, nurturing a commitment to achieving your goal and becoming able to help yourself when you feel distressed. It's a toolbox that contains ways to keep yourself safe, stay within your *window of tolerance*, respect your boundaries, use journaling to gain perspective on your rejection sensitivity, self-soothe, and explore the five domains of self-awareness that make up *STEAM*. That's the acronym I referenced in the introduction and will describe further at the end of this chapter and in detail throughout the book.

ASSESSING HOW STABLE YOU FEEL

People need to feel some measure of stability in their lives in order to take on the additional challenge of making personal changes, including becoming more resilient to rejection. So, it is essential that you take care of the fundamental activities of daily living, such as stocking your home with healthy food and paying the bills.

> Katrina is a teacher's aide at the local elementary school. She was essentially "trained" to take care of others by growing up with alcoholic parents, who left the care of her younger siblings to her—something she remembers doing since she was about seven years old. To this day, *How can I help?* immediately comes to mind any time she has even the briefest pause of activity in her life. She feels so driven to care for family and friends that she is always doing things for them, to the point of regularly forgoing sleep or eating meals so that she can bake for them, look up information about their medical issues, or be there to talk with them when they are upset. Even the thought of wanting to say no or not do *all* she can to help makes her feel unworthy and leaves her with an underlying fear of them dismissing her from their lives.
>
> Whenever it occurs to her that she is chronically unhappy, exhausted, and wants to take better care of herself, she immediately scolds, *Stop being so selfish!* Though she senses that it's important to change, she falls back to *I'm just too tired and*

hungry to even think about it. Then she does what she always does—push herself to help others, ignoring her own needs.

All people have limited inner strength and resources. So, to have the energy and develop the ability to overcome your sensitivity to rejection, you must first meet your basic needs sufficiently.

Are You Taking Care of Your Basic Needs?

This exercise will help you assess whether you would benefit from giving your basic needs more attention. To complete it, you'll need just a pencil and your journal, or a piece of paper.

Copy any of the sentences below that you basically agree with.

Safe Living Situation

- I feel physically or emotionally intimidated at home.
- My home environment is not emotionally healthy.
- My living situation is not stable.

Financial Security

- I do not have sufficient income that I can depend upon.
- I am not able to afford basic bills.
- I do not feel capable of managing my finances.

Basic Health Needs

- I do not get sufficient sleep.
- I have significant concerns regarding my eating habits or diet.
- I do not get sufficient exercise.
- I do not go to a physician when I feel ill.
- I do not get annual physical checkups.

Consider how each of the topics you copied affects your sense of safety and security. Think about how they might be undermining your ability to think clearly and to focus on and address your rejection sensitivity.

Make a plan to address any areas of concern. For each one, it might help to label a separate page with the topic and list some concrete steps to address it. Make the steps small enough that you are likely to do them. For instance, if you have trouble managing finances, you might plan to take one small action each day, such as assembling your bills in a pile, sorting them by type of bill (e.g., water, electricity), and making a file to place the sorted bills in.

If you feel like this is more than you can do, get help. You might ask a friend or reach out to a professional, such as an accountant or a financial planner. By supporting your basic needs, you are giving yourself the core strength to begin working on overcoming your sensitivity to rejection.

STAYING IN YOUR WINDOW OF TOLERANCE

> *Stop overreacting. Linda is just enjoying time with her friends,* Chad thought reassuringly, bringing himself back from the brink of an emotional abyss. *Just because she's talking more with them isn't a statement that she's done with me.* He was using this opportunity at a party to work on trying to stay within his *window of tolerance.* In the beginning of their relationship, his window was small— even a hint of possible rejection might put him outside of it. But as he repeatedly responded to this by calming and focusing himself, he found that he increased his tolerance for addressing rejection. In other words, by expanding this window, he was becoming less distressed by, and better able to handle, perceived rejections.

Noted psychiatrist Dr. Dan Siegel (2010) describes the *window of tolerance* as a range of arousal that you need to be within to function well, such as being able to effectively receive and process information (shown in Figure 2.1). But given your sensitivity to rejection, remaining in that window when you feel rejected, or fear it, can take some work. As Chad did, you can expand this window by learning to respect your limits, soothe yourself when you become highly upset, and yet still challenge yourself to face your emotional struggles with rejection.

Figure 2.1 Window of Tolerance

When people feel threatened by rejection, they are cast outside their window of tolerance. Their brains try to protect them from this pain in one of two ways, through *hyper-arousal* (too much arousal) or *hypo-arousal* (too little arousal). Hyper-arousal involves going into fight-or-flight mode, and hypo-arousal is characterized by shutting down.

As an example of hyper-arousal, consider this scenario:

When Chad first met Linda, he was immediately attracted to her, but when she glanced down at her phone while he was talking, the sense of rejection hit him like a body blow. He quickly became *hyper-aroused* and flooded by an intensity he could feel in his body. No stranger to this sense of hyper-arousal, he felt overcome by intense fear and anxiety. As always happened when he was in this state, he became preoccupied with the thought that he was going to be rejected. He was outside the window of tolerance and couldn't think clearly. So, he was unable to learn to cope differently with rejection, because learning *in general* can't happen here.

The opposite way your brain might try to protect you is through *hypo-arousal,* or shutting down. In this state, you would likely feel emotionally disconnected or depressed. You might move less and feel out of touch with your body. Your mind might also feel sluggish, making it difficult to think. Sometimes people speak of significant events, such as being fired from a job, with the same nonchalance that they talk about the weather.

It's not unusual that when a therapy patient begins to talk about deep feelings of being unworthy or not mattering to others, they aren't consciously upset. Instead, they might suddenly get tired or have trouble thinking clearly. These are signs of hypo-arousal, which is a serious obstacle to change.

While working through your issues of rejection, you will undoubtedly end up outside of your window of tolerance at different times. That's to be expected. Many of the exercises in the chapters on developing self-awareness in the domains of STEAM (sensations, thoughts, emotions, actions, and mentalizing) are designed to help bring you back to a more optimal level of arousal.

RESPECTING YOUR BOUNDARIES

You may find that even consciously thinking about the topic of rejection sends your anxiety level through the roof, well outside your window of tolerance. You may react to this by being critical of yourself, such as by thinking, *You are so oversensitive! What is your problem that you still worry so much about what other people think of you?!* Your desire to feel stronger and be more resilient is admirable, but chastising yourself will make you defensive and lead you to fear the rebuke, along with the original fear of rejection. There is a better way.

Rather than chastising yourself, respect your feelings, which are based on your life experiences. Approach yourself more slowly, taking the time to understand your fears and struggles, appreciate and encourage your efforts, and absorb the support you are giving yourself. This can more effectively—and compassionately—help alleviate your sensitivity to rejection.

Consider this analogy: You come across a neglected dog in an alley and you decide to help him. As you approach him, he slowly backs away and begins to growl. Understanding that he feels threatened, you stop walking and just stand there. After a time, he seems to relax, but keeps a constant eye on you. You bring water and food, but again he will not let you approach. So, you put down the bowl and back away. He slowly goes to the food and water. With time, the dog feels safe enough to let you sit as he eats and drinks. He lets you pet him. Finally, you can take him home, groom him, and enjoy your new friend!

This slow, gentle approach can be a very frustrating process. I've had many patients become angry with themselves for being overly distressed by rejection or fighting the process of change, even though they consciously want to improve their lives. But when that happens, it can help to take a step back and think. If experience has taught you that you are in that much danger, it would be natural to resist letting down your guard.

So, when you try to work on this issue and find that you are quick to feel overly distressed or guarded, remember the importance of respecting that reaction. Again, it's the result of what you've learned from previous experiences. If you don't think you need that reaction any longer, then an important part of changing is to gently, but firmly and repeatedly, offer yourself the nurturance and encouragement necessary to free yourself from your rejection sensitivity. You can do this through the information and exercises in this book.

Note: If you have a history of childhood neglect or physical, sexual, or emotional abuse, you may really need the help of a trained professional to guide you through the process of accepting and having self-compassion for these struggles.

JOURNALING TO YOUR ADVANTAGE

Many people find journaling a valuable tool for getting a new perspective on their struggles with feeling rejection—or any other life challenge, for that matter. The acts of composing your thoughts, writing them down, and then rereading them frequently help people organize, clarify, and gain perspective on their experiences. Also, reading your entry later can remind you of forgotten insights.

Journaling can be completed in both structured and unstructured ways, and each one offers different benefits. Structured journaling is writing in response to a prompt. It may be an open-ended question, such as "Are there common situations in your relationships that tend to trigger you to feel rejected (e.g., you are not invited out with other friends)?" Or the prompt may offer more detailed directions, such as "Write about your emotional reactions to rejection. Then write about your behavioral reactions. Finally, write about how these reactions affect other people." Throughout this book, you will see the suggestion to reflect on various topics. Consider each of these to be a possible journaling prompt.

Unstructured journaling is writing out your thoughts without specific directions or with only a basic topic in mind. It can feel very liberating. One powerful way to do this is by writing with a stream-of-consciousness style. You write what comes to mind without concern for grammar, spelling, editing, or even making sense. In other words, you just let whatever comes to mind pour out onto the paper. By expressing your raw experience without intellectualizing or being limited by what "makes sense," you open yourself to everything that's happening within. This can help you experience some catharsis and gain insights about yourself and your perceptions of the world.

There may be times when you want to add some more reflective thinking to this journaling. Reread what you wrote—either immediately or later—and journal about your thoughts and insights. The process of unstructured journaling—with or without the second look—may provide some clarity, so I strongly encourage you to do this periodically during your journey of personal growth.

It can be particularly helpful to use one journal for all of your notes and written responses to exercises in this book. This will give you an opportunity to revisit and reflect on old entries. In the process, you might remind yourself of forgotten insights, find that your thinking has changed, or just get yourself back on track with a previous line of thinking. Looking back over your growth from doing this work might also encourage you—it can be easy to get stuck focusing on where you are falling short, failing to recognize how far you have come.

I have had a number of patients hesitate to keep a journal because they don't want anyone to see it. If this is the case for you, there are a couple of things you can do. You can keep it in a place that is safe from prying eyes (and maybe even lock it up). Or you can write out your thoughts and then throw out the paper. This obviously won't allow you to review it later, but the process of physically writing your thoughts is worthwhile in itself. Finally, you might prefer to type your thoughts on a computer (tablet, laptop, desktop, phone, whatever). While this can work, consider that you may find that you connect more emotionally with the process by writing out your thoughts by hand.

LEARNING TO SELF-SOOTHE

It's unrealistic to expect to feel calm the whole time you are working on freeing yourself from your sensitivity to rejection. However, when you are so upset that you can't think straight or respond in a constructive way, your first priority needs to be soothing yourself and bringing your arousal level back within your window of tolerance (a concept described earlier in this chapter).

For this reason, it is important that you know ways that you can rely on to soothe yourself when distressed.

Create a Self-Soothing "Go-To" List

Use this exercise to create a list that you can refer to when you feel upset. It's important to write down a list of these activities while you are calm so that you don't have to dream them up when you need them most—remember, the more upset you are, the harder it is to think. You may want to complete this exercise on your phone or a loose piece of paper, rather than in your journal, so that you can more easily take the list with you.

On your list, note activities you find calming. Think about the activities you engage in now. Also, think back on activities you used to do and would be interested in returning to.

Add activities from the list below. Check to see if this list reminds you of activities you engage in to self-soothe. You might also decide to try out new activities.

- Listening to music

- Taking a hot bath or shower

- Exercising

- Doing yoga

- Talking with a friend

- Reading

- Playing games on your phone

- Surfing the Internet

- Watching a movie or show

- Doing a craft

- Playing an instrument

- Eating a comfort food (best to do this slowly so you can savor it)

- Getting a massage

- Doing something that makes you laugh

When you are done with your list, be sure to keep it in an easily accessible place. You can always add to the list or even make notes about new activities you have yet to try in times of stress.

Review the list periodically. The more you reflect on, update, and reference the list, the more likely you will think to use it when you feel upset.

You may notice any activity that helps you can also be *over*done, making it problematic. So, you need to monitor when, or for how long, you engage in these activities. If certain ones tend to become self-destructive—such as emotional eating or surfing the Internet—then it may be best to steer clear of them totally, or at certain times (e.g., not eating snacks after 8 p.m.).

Learning Relaxation Exercises

There are many exercises that are specifically meant to help people relax. Below is a list of some that you might benefit from learning, or from being reminded of.

Visualization: Close your eyes and think about a setting that you find especially comforting, such as the woods or a beach. Using as many of your senses as you can, imagine what it would be like to actually be there. For instance, you might choose the beach and imagine feeling the warmth of the sun on your face, hearing the sound of the ocean, watching the seagulls flying overhead, and even smelling and tasting the salt in the air.

Deep or diaphragmatic breathing: As you breathe in through your nose, allow your belly to fill like a balloon. Then as you exhale, your belly will deflate. Note that your lungs will not move much. Take five or ten slow breaths. It can help to place one hand on your stomach and your other one on your chest to guide your breathing. If you have trouble doing this, lie on your back with your feet flat on the floor (so that your knees are bent). This position makes it easier to do diaphragmatic breathing. After you get the hang of it, you will be able to do it while sitting up.

Square breathing: This is helpful for people whose thoughts are racing, keeping them distressed. As you engage in deep breathing, count to 4 as you inhale, pause to the count of 4, exhale to the count of 4, and finally hold to the count of 4. If you are a visual person, imagine drawing each side of a square as you count and breathe.

In addition to these exercises, you might find developing a mindfulness or meditation practice can help you calm down, along with enjoying other benefits.

The Many Ways You Can Benefit from Mindfulness

Renowned mindfulness teacher Jon Kabat-Zinn defines mindfulness in his book, *Wherever You Go, There You Are* as "paying attention in a particular way: on purpose, in the present moment, and nonjudgmentally" (1994, 4). You can attend to any aspect of your experience, such as your sensations, thoughts, emotions, or actions.

Much research has shown that when people learn to consciously pay attention to their experiences without judgment, they benefit in many ways, such as:

- Increased tolerance and modulation of emotions, including fear

- Stress reduction

- Better self-control

- Improved focus

- Less emotional reactivity

- Increased mental flexibility

- More self-insight

- Greater compassion

- Greater satisfaction in relationships

You can apply mindfulness to helping reduce your sensitivity to rejection by bringing your awareness to it. Rather than being driven by your emotional reactivity to rejection, with mindful awareness you will be able to think more clearly about your rejection experiences, or fears of them. As a result, you will be able to respond in healthier ways. Later chapters will include mindfulness exercises to help you increase self-awareness in the five domains of STEAM, which are described in the next section.

BUILDING SELF-AWARENESS WITH STEAM

As explained earlier in this chapter, your hypersensitivity to rejection and abandonment (including your fear of them) reveals a problem based in your attachment style. That is, your model of self probably involves perceiving yourself less positively and more toward being unlovable, unworthy, inadequate, flawed, or some similar experience. In addition, your model of others probably involves seeing them, to some significant degree, as not truly empathic and supportive of you.

An important step toward improving your sense of security is getting to know yourself better through increased self-awareness. As you do this, you can also reassess your model of others and work toward being more open to the love and acceptance they have to offer. Each of the next five chapters guides you through increasing self-awareness in a different domain, collectively called STEAM, which stands for sensations, thoughts, emotions, actions, and mentalization.

Sensations: As you learn to pay attention to your body, you will find that you respond to experiences on a physical level. If you tend to be out of touch with your emotions, tuning in to your sensations can be a doorway into a fuller awareness of your feelings.

Thoughts: People often have thoughts without reflecting on them. By learning to observe your thoughts and think about them, you will begin to understand them in a new way. This includes gaining insight into how they relate to your sensations, emotions, and actions.

Emotions: Increasing self-awareness of your emotions is like shining a light on them, enabling you to better see the ones that were obscured in the shadows of your awareness, as well as discovering emotions you did not realize were even there. The more you pay attention to all of your emotions, the more fully you can acknowledge them, tolerate them, and even appreciate them. You will ultimately come to value and have compassion for your "true" or "authentic" self.

Actions: By paying attention to your actions, you can learn a lot about how they relate to your thoughts and emotions, and how they frequently reinforce your negative self-perceptions and struggles with rejection.

Mentalization: Psychoanalyst Peter Fonagy and his colleagues have elaborated (though not originated) this psychological concept, which is linked to Bowlby's theory of attachment (Allen, Bleiberg, and Haslam-Hopwood 2003; Fonagy and Target 1997). It describes the mainly unconscious way that people "get" where they and others are "coming from." They do this by understanding how people's inner experiences affect their actions. This enables them to be empathic and compassionate toward others and themselves. So, when you develop this ability, you are strengthening a positive sense of yourself and a sense that significant people in your life will be accepting and supportive of you. Along with those changes, you will also lessen your struggles with rejection.

The self-awareness of STEAM is an ability you develop with practice and experience. This involves moving back and forth among the different domains of awareness. So, while you work in a chapter to develop one domain of awareness, you can expect to revisit exercises from the chapters on other domains of awareness that you have already completed. As you get more experienced in doing this, you will find that you can move more easily among the different domains, which will give you a fuller, richer sense of yourself. While no one reaches a state of full and continuous self-awareness, you can learn skills to regularly tap into yourself. The more you do this, the more it will characterize how you relate to yourself.

Caution: You may sometimes find that increasing your awareness intensifies your reactions to rejection. When this happens, take a break from the exercise or exercises that seem to trigger these reactions. You might find it helpful to spotlight areas that nurture more positive feelings about yourself. You can do this by completing some of the exercises in chapter 8, "Building Self-Acceptance." As you become more open to changing, you may find it helpful to try the exercises in chapter 9, "Nurturing Compassionate Self-Awareness."

With these tools for nurturing openness, sensitivity, and commitment to change, you can effectively apply yourself to addressing, and moving past, your struggles with rejection. Essential to this process is increasing your self-awareness in the five domains of STEAM, which will start with the next chapter, "Sensations."

CHAPTER 3

Sensations

Chad, now twenty-four years old, reflects on his days as a state champion baseball pitcher in high school, and as an athlete. Back then he learned to hone his physical conditioning: eating well; getting sufficient sleep; and building his strength, agility, and endurance through working out. *But that was a long time ago,* Chad thinks. *And, even though I was in great shape, I really had no clue who I was—or even what my body was telling me.*

Now, years later, Chad is learning to pay attention to his body in a way he never did before. At first, he doesn't recognize that his breathing becomes shallow while trying to interpret a text from his girlfriend Linda in the same way his breathing would grow short back in his baseball days, while pitching with runners on base. Though the source of anxiety and fear could hardly be more different, his physical reaction is the same. But then he remembers how his pitching coach used to direct him to be aware of changes in his breathing and take a deep breath. *Just focus on my breathing. Take a slow, deep breath in…And exhale.* As he lets air slowly escape his mouth, he can already feel his anxiety ease. With a few breaths, he calms enough to be able to reflect on what is going on. He realizes how his tense breathing was prompted by a fear that, when Linda said she was not able to meet for lunch, it meant she was going to leave him. *Boy, am I overreacting,* he thinks. With another deep breath, he reminds himself, *I know I'm worried, but she did tell me she wants to reschedule for tomorrow.*

Many people think of their bodies as separate from their inner selves. Rather than attending to their sensations—the "S" in STEAM—as a message about their personal experience, they view their bodies as they would an external object. This is even true for those who treat their body as a temple, attending carefully and thoughtfully to its many needs, such as sleep, nutrition, and exercise. While they nurture their physical selves, they do not listen to the messages their bodies send about their inner experiences—such as Chad did when he realized that his shallow breathing was the result of his fear of rejection. Other people barely register their bodies and physical sensations, focusing instead on enhancing their intellectual or spiritual selves. Even many who understand the importance of their physical *and* inner experiences attend to them separately—as though their bodies were not connected to their inner selves. They don't fully acknowledge or appreciate the connection between the mind and body.

The mind-body connection is not only real, but it is also powerful. Your body has its own level of experience and speaks its own language, especially through your sensations. When you are open to listening, you can tap into yourself in a fuller and richer way. For instance, sensing heat in your face might relate to having self-critical thoughts and feeling embarrassed about your actions. You might also feel an incredible churning in your stomach that tells you that your embarrassment is intense. So, by tuning in to your body, you can get to know *you* better.

People carry some experiences in them on a nonverbal, physical level. So, they cannot immediately think about these experiences because there are no words for them. As an example, children who are neglected or whose emotions are regularly criticized by attachment figures learn that they are inadequate or unlovable. This can even happen in everyday kinds of ways, such as being sent to their rooms every time they cry or express distress. For them, the message that their emotional selves don't matter is just part of being—not something they've been expressly told or that they have put words to. Yet, they perceive something is wrong with them through a sense of disconnection with their bodies, as well as with their emotions.

To whatever degree your struggles with rejection are conscious or unconscious, paying attention to your sensations can be a helpful first step toward addressing them. These are raw experiences you can learn to observe, experience, and then use as a portal into your inner world. As such, they are important in building self-awareness, along with the other domains of STEAM.

The information and exercises in this chapter offer opportunities for you to learn to relate to your sensations in ways that will increase your self-awareness. There are suggestions and exercises that can help you connect more with your current sensations, enabling you to attend to them and to how they might be delivering messages from your inner self. The next couple of sections—"Increasing Your Bodily Awareness" and "Mindfulness Meditation"—are two examples of this. You are also invited to allow your body to express nonverbal experiences through the creative arts in the section "Tapping Your Raw Experience with Creative Arts" and its related exercise, "Create a Personal Collage." Other exercises use your sensations to calm you and to remain grounded in the present, rather than being consumed by memories of past—or fears of future—rejection. Finally, the sections that follow will enable you to use your physical sensations as a doorway to your other domains of STEAM.

INCREASING YOUR BODILY AWARENESS

In expecting rejection from others, you may devote yourself to chasing approval or trying to achieve a sense of worth by meeting unrealistically high standards. These responses are similar in that they both focus outwardly, away from your inner distress. This may leave you—as it does for many people—so disconnected from your body that you don't fully register your physical self.

Being out of touch with your sensations may help keep your distress at arm's length, but it can also leave you restlessly or anxiously unhappy—registering a vague awareness that something is not quite right, but being unable to put your finger on it. Many people who operate this way end up with physical problems, such as headaches, chest pain, or upset stomach. Their stress might also lead to or exacerbate more serious medical issues, such as high blood pressure, heart disease, diabetes, or irritable bowel syndrome. In addition to having these problems, they are less likely to respond to symptoms, such as not seeking medical help when they have chest pains. In all of these circumstances, learning to listen to your body is a first step toward responding to your personal needs.

I have seen some patients who are so disconnected from their physical bodies that they don't even know they are upset until I point out a tear running down their cheek. Even then, they may not realize they are sad. Any insights about their struggles tend to remain intellectual. While thoughts and feelings influence each other, they operate—to a large degree—separately in the brain. So, people cannot simply *think* their way out of emotions. (You learn this each time you unsuccessfully command yourself, *Stop being upset!*) But reconnecting with their bodies provides an experiential connection to their emotions that they can then reflect upon.

To nurture this bodily awareness, it is helpful to build practices into your life that can connect you with your body. Some suggestions are listed below.

Get moving and pay attention: This can mean strolling around your neighborhood, going to the gym, playing a sport, hiking, or even doing active chores around the house, such as cleaning out cabinets, gardening, or raking leaves. Pay attention to how your body feels. You might notice that your poor posture is causing your lower back to hurt. Or you might notice that the aches you feel as you start your hike disappear as your muscles warm up. Be sure to take note of any such positive feelings that accompany your body getting exercise.

Massage: As you get a massage, pay attention to how it feels when various muscle groups are being worked. You might also notice particular emotions arising. Simply observe the different sensations and emotions.

Dancing: Being in touch with your body is inherent to dancing. Given your struggles with relationships, you might gain an added benefit by doing dances that involve a partner, such as ballroom dancing, salsa, or square dancing. There are also many health benefits to dancing, such as improving your aerobic fitness, coordination, and self-confidence.

Singing: Belting out a song requires awareness of your breath and body. Importantly, it releases a hormone called oxytocin, which can reduce stress and anxiety while also increasing trust and a sense of connection. So, if you sing with a group, you can get an added feel-good from connecting on a nonverbal level, as well as being socially connected.

Yoga: Yoga involves awareness of your breath and body. It also offers certain poses intended for helping people feel grounded, or being present in their body.

Tai chi: Originally developed in China as a form of self-defense, tai chi is "meditation in motion" and facilitates a sense of calm. It offers gentle exercise, including stretching.

Martial arts: Aikido, karate, kickboxing, mixed martial arts, and tae kwon do require bodily awareness, such as awareness of breathing, focus, and a balance between muscular tension and relaxation. They require a kinesthetic awareness as moves are performed. They also have the added benefits of teaching self-defense and building confidence.

In addition to these methods of reconnecting with your bodily sensations, you might consider meditation. This is explored in the next sections, and exercises for different ways to practice it are also suggested.

MINDFULNESS MEDITATION

Mindfulness meditation is a practice that ultimately increases your connection with, and acceptance of, yourself. It also fosters calmness and a positive state of mind. You can use different techniques to nonjudgmentally attend to your experiences, including all the domains of STEAM (though this chapter specifically focuses on sensations). For instance, as described fully in the next section, you might focus on the sensation of breathing, repeatedly bringing your attention back to it when you get distracted. Practicing this at times when you are relatively calm can help prepare you for mindful awareness of more distressing experiences, such as when your heart beats quickly. By increasing your mindful awareness of sensations, you can experience them without being overwhelmed or reactive. When your sensations relate to rejection, you can tolerate and appreciate them, enabling you to reflect on them and develop a healthier response.

While you can learn a lot about meditation from the Internet, make sure—as you would be wise to do researching any subject—that the information you are getting is valid. Some well-respected teachers of mindfulness are Jack Kornfield, Matthieu Ricard, Joseph Goldstein, Sharon Salzberg, Tara Brach, and His Holiness the 14th Dalai Lama. You might also want to explore the work at UCLA's Mindful Awareness Research Center or the work of Jon Kabat-Zinn and his Mindfulness-Based Stress Reduction (MBSR), which has been shown to be very effective. If you are interested in the neurological basis of meditation, check out the work of Rick Hanson and Dan Siegel. Because mindfulness and meditation have proliferated, there are many more teachers whose work is worth exploring.

Mindful Breathing Meditation

One common way to begin meditating is with a mindful breathing meditation. Many people find that simply maintaining a regular meditation practice of mindful breathing helps them effectively calm themselves during stressful times, including when they experience rejection. While it can be tempting to just use mindful breathing when you are upset, this as-needed approach—while often potentially helpful—may not be as effective in calming you as when you maintain a regular practice. It also misses out on the benefits of increasing mindful self-awareness even during less stressful times.

If you decide to develop a meditation practice, choose a designated time each day. As a beginner, you might choose to sit for 2 or 3 minutes a day. As you gain more experience, you can increase the time—but do so slowly! It's better to meditate for only a few minutes a day as a regular practice than to struggle with a more ambitious amount of time that you give up after just a few days. You also want to choose an amount of time that is comfortably available to you. (Stressing about getting to the next thing on your to-do list is counterproductive.) As you become more comfortable and experienced with this meditation and feel motivated by its benefits, you can increase to a practice of 15 or 20 minutes once or twice a day.

Learn to Breathe Mindfully

It's important to spend some time preparing before you begin a mindful breathing meditation session.

Preparation

Timer: For this exercise, you can use any timer, including the one on your phone. However, some people like to use meditation apps that offer meditation bells.

Location: Although breathing mindfully can help you anyplace, a breathing meditation needs to be done in a quiet location where you will not be interrupted.

State of mind: Begin by choosing to focus solely on mindful breathing. No multitasking. Commit yourself to being "in" the experience as opposed to thinking about it.

Position: You can sit comfortably on a chair or on the floor with your legs crossed. Rest your hands on your lap and make sure you sit up straight. If you are not comfortable with closing your eyes, you can look downward so that you are not distracted by anything in your environment. Another option is to lie down on the floor and close your eyes.

Breathing Meditation

Simply focus on breathing naturally (not trying to slow the breath or do anything with it). Notice your bodily sensations related to breathing, such as the air coming in through your nostrils and the rise and fall of your chest and belly. When you notice that your mind has wandered, gently observe this—perhaps even saying "wandering" to yourself—and return your attention to your breathing.

When your timer goes off, bring your attention back to the room you are in. Do this slowly, giving yourself the time you need to reorient.

When you have completed this meditation, allow yourself to appreciate that you have nurtured yourself in this way.

If you struggle with constant worries or thoughts while trying to breathe mindfully, you might find it helpful to direct your thinking. You can say "inhale" and "exhale" in your mind as you breathe. Or you can count your breaths. After some practice, you may find that you no long need to direct your thinking in this way, and you can refocus on the sensations of breathing.

Walking Meditation

A great way to ground your body is with a walking meditation. This common meditation practice helps focus your attention and bring an inner calm as you increase your sense of connection and embodied awareness.

The practice involves being fully aware of your experience as you walk. For this reason, it is best to choose a quiet place and an undisturbed time where you can give it your whole attention. Walk for whatever length of time feels right to you, perhaps increasing the time as you get more comfortable with the practice. It is often helpful to begin the practice without a destination, as you might feel pressured to get there. Instead, choose an area where you can walk back and forth or on a circular path. I have personally appreciated walking in a labyrinth. Also, you might want to try this out at home or where there are no people who might be watching.

Before you even begin, take a few slow, deep breaths. Then walk. It often helps to walk slowly, but you can walk at any pace as long as you maintain your mindful awareness. Observe the sensations on the bottoms of your feet, as pressure moves from your heel to your toes. Note the shift of weight from one leg to the other as you step forward.

When you observe your thoughts wandering off on their own path, acknowledge it and then gently return them to your body. You can expect this to happen many times. Noted meditation teacher Jack Kornfield (2008) articulately offers common meditation advice when he says in *The Wise Heart*, "Like training a puppy, you will need to come back a thousand times."

As you get more experienced with this, you might also choose to open your awareness to other sensations. Note the sights, sounds, and smells. Be open to all of your experiences. But when your mind wanders to reflecting on them or just takes a different path altogether, again, observe this distraction and gently guide your awareness back to your bodily sensations.

Being Mindfully Aware of Your Sensations

In addition to practicing awareness of chosen sensations—as with the mindful breathing and mindful walking practices—you can benefit from allowing the target of your awareness to arise from broadly attending to your whole body. Our sensations often deliver messages that tell us about ourselves. However, these communications can only help us if we pick them up and read them. For this reason, it is crucial that we are aware of, and attend to, our physical experiences—as Chad did when he realized that his tight chest and difficulty breathing were signs of his fear of rejection by Linda. You can learn more about tapping your sensations to increase self-awareness by watching my brief video *Sensations: Getting to Know Your Rejection Sensitivity* at www.drbecker-phelps.com/home/bouncing-back/ or http://www.newharbinger.com/44024.

As important as it is to attend to your body, it is also crucial that you put that awareness in context, especially if you—like many people—feel distressed by signs of anxiety or other physical sensations. Be aware of your reactions to your sensations and consider whether your reactions fit the situation, or whether you might be overreacting. For instance, if you feel a wave of light-headedness while at the gym, you might realize that it's likely related to fears of having to give a presentation later that day, rather than assuming that you have a serious medical condition. If you tend to react emotionally to your awareness of certain sensations, you might want to turn to the "Assessing Your Current Situation" section of chapter 7, "Mentalizing." That chapter, as a whole, also addresses in depth how to guide your responses to the different domains of awareness.

Reconnect with Your Senses

When you fear rejection or are feeling rejected, find a quiet place to sit. Although it's up to you to decide how long to do this exercise, make sure you will not be disturbed for at least 10 minutes.

Choose to focus on your body. You may find it helps to slowly scan from the bottom of your feet to the top of your head. Stop at any point where you are aware of sensations. Make note of each sensation before moving on. You might notice that your stomach is unsettled, your chest feels tight, there is a lump in your throat, or there are tears in your eyes.

Allow your attention to be pulled to one of your sensations. Attend to it without trying to change it. As you stay with the sensation, you might notice that it changes on its own. That's okay. Just keep paying attention. If you have difficulty identifying your sensations because you feel numb, then pay attention to that. When you get distracted, remind yourself to refocus on your body. Expect that you will need to do this many times.

The whole point of this exercise is simply to practice tuning in to your sensations. Because being mindfully aware of those sensations can be particularly difficult to do as you challenge yourself in working through this book, you may find it helpful to return to this exercise at different points along your journey (and various sections in the upcoming chapters make this suggestion).

Engaging in a daily practice connecting with your senses can be particularly helpful in reconnecting with your physical body and learning to "hear" what it is telling you. As your ability to do this improves, you will probably notice certain emotions rising up. At this point, review the "The Importance of Connecting with Your Emotions" section of chapter 5, "Emotions." Then you might want to try the other exercises in that section.

TAPPING YOUR RAW EXPERIENCE WITH CREATIVE ARTS

Your sensations—whether you are aware of it or not—embody the experiences of your inner self, including your struggles with rejection. It is a connection that is beyond words, and so it can be difficult to think about. However, you may find that you can tap into, and express, your embodied inner self through the creative arts. In doing so, you will discover valuable personal truths held deep within, much like unlocking a treasure chest.

For instance, an artist might feel compelled to draw a picture rife with symbolism for their inner turmoil. By itself, this can feel palpably relieving and calming. But the sensation of releasing this creative energy can also enable the conscious mind to make sense of an embodied experience it had only obliquely perceived, or possibly never even knew existed.

The creative process comes more easily for some people than others. If you are comfortable with a particular art form or have an interest in one, you might explore it as a way to learn more about yourself. For instance, you might decide to explore the visual arts, such as drawing, painting, sculpting, animation, photography, or video. Or perhaps you are drawn to the performing arts, such as dance, music, acting, comedy, dramatic recitation, or mime. Whatever your interest, remember that you're pursuing it for the purpose of self-exploration. That means rather than just mastering techniques, your focus will be more on self-expression.

While the creative arts can help you connect with your raw experience and true self, using the arts for deep personal expression can feel intimidating. This is especially true when you hold an image of what your work "should" look or sound like. So, it is important to focus more on the process of creating art than on judging the outcome of your work.

In expressing your embodied self, you will more fully appreciate pleasant and joyful experiences, while being more present for painful ones. When you express that pain, you are validating its existence in a way that may make it easier to reflect on, empathize with, and have compassion for your pain. As someone who fears rejection, sharing your artwork can be particularly difficult. However, if you take that risk with supportive others, who can then empathize with your experience, you open yourself to the possibility of feeling "held," validated, and no longer alone in it. By definition, the relationship (or attachment) will be more secure, leaving you less fearful of being ignored, dismissed, or abandoned.

Create a Personal Collage

There is no one correct way to create a collage, but this exercise is specifically designed to encourage you to listen to your inner, nonverbal self. It encourages you to let you body "talk." As you engage in this process, pay attention to what you are feeling and to any particular thoughts or insights that might come to you. With this in mind, read through these directions before starting.

Assemble the materials you will need. Be prepared with glue, scissors, and magazines that you can freely cut up. Choose a piece of paper or poster board that you will glue pictures to—the size is completely up to you.

Prepare your workspace. You want a surface with sufficient space and seating that is comfortable.

Prepare your mind. Before you begin, you might want to take a few deep breaths to bring you into the moment.

Clip images. As you flip through the magazines, cut out any images that attract your attention. If you find yourself lost in thought and distracted at any point, bring your attention back to browsing the magazines. The idea is to let your interest in an image "happen to you" rather than looking for something in particular.

In addition to pictures, certain words, colors, or designs might jump out at you. Whatever it is that grabs you, cut it out. None of this needs to make sense. However, if you are aware of certain thoughts or feelings that accompany your interest in the picture, consciously allow for them. (You might even jot down a few notes so that you can journal about them later.)

Affix your images to the paper. You might glue down the cutouts as you go, or after you have a stack of them in front of you. Just as with deciding what to clip from the magazines, glue them down in a way that feels right.

Sit back and appreciate your work. This is a time to just absorb the visual artwork you have created. Resist any impulse to critique it.

After you have finished, put the collage someplace where you are likely to see it. Sometimes, rather than having some new awareness hit you while you are working, an insight seeps its way into your consciousness as you observe the collage later.

HOW YOUR SELF-CRITICISM EXPRESSES ITSELF IN YOUR SENSATIONS

People who tend to expect rejection also struggle with being self-critical. They play the roles of being both critic and victim. By paying attention to your bodily sensations when you are engaged in thinking from each of these perspectives, you can gain greater self-awareness and enrich your self-understanding. Then you might naturally respond more kindly to yourself or feel motivated to work on doing this.

Use Your Sensations to Explore Your Self-Criticism

When you are aware of being self-critical, sit in a quiet place with your journal or a pad of paper and pencil. Make sure you will not be disturbed for at least 20 minutes.

Make two columns on the paper. Title them "Critic" and "Victim."

Take a few slow, deep breaths to ground yourself in the moment. This can help bring your full attention to this exercise.

Attend to the self-criticism, identifying with the harsh voice that is speaking: your critical self. As you do this, have that voice address yourself as a separate person, using "you" instead of "I."

Choose to shift your focus to your body, noting any sensations. You may find it helpful to close your eyes as you do this. After you have a good grasp of sensations that arise or feel heightened in response to this angry self, list them under the "Critic" column.

It's easy to get carried away by your angry thoughts, so don't be surprised if it happens. Simply remind yourself to refocus on your body—you may need to repeat this guidance several times.

Return your attention to these physical sensations, attending to whatever emotions seem connected with them. List these emotions in the "Critic" column, too.

Now attend to the same self-criticism, but identify with being the victim. Now you are on the receiving end of the attack. What is your victim voice saying?

Again, shift your focus to your body, noting your sensations. After identifying sensations that have arisen or are heightened by feeling attacked, list them under the "Victim" column. Again, any time you get distracted, refocus on your body.

Return your attention to these physical sensations, attending to whatever emotions seem connected to them. Note these on the chart in the "Victim" column.

Disconnect from the exercise. Take several slow, deep breaths or even walk away for a few minutes.

Review what you've written and reflect on your experience of doing this exercise. You might find it helpful to journal about the relationship between the critic and victim aspects of yourself and how they affect you in general.

To help you understand how you can use your sensations to gain insight about your self-criticism, look at Chad's responses to this exercise.

Attend to the self-criticism, identifying with the harsh voice that is speaking: your critical self. Chad recognized that he was being harsh with himself even as he thought, *You are such an idiot for forgetting about the meeting with your boss today. Now she is going to hate you.*

Following the next couple of steps in the exercise, he completed the "Critic" column of the chart with his sensations and emotions.

Now attend to the same self-criticism, but identify with being the victim. Chad was conscious of a part of himself that felt attacked by his self-criticism. It said, *You're right. I am an idiot. Now she knows it, too, and she is going to fire me.*

At this point, he completed the directions related to the "Victim" column.

Critic	Victim
Tension in my chest	Nauseated
Clenching my jaw	Tearing up
Heat rising in me	Afraid, ashamed, sad, defeated
Angry, frustrated	

After disconnecting from the exercise, Chad had a lot to think about. He could see how his assumption that people were going to disapprove of him led to viewing himself harshly, and that he just spiraled down from there.

The immediate purpose of the last exercise is to help you use bodily awareness to be more aware of the critic and victim voices and experiences within you. Notice how the same self-criticism can elicit and feed different sensations and emotions on the different lists. Chad's thoughts that he was incompetent were associated with tension and anger on his critic list, but associated with tears and sadness on his victim list. The goal of expanding your awareness in this way is to help you go beyond just living the experiences to being able to reflect upon them.

If you can connect with your sensations but have difficulty labeling your emotions, you might want to put this exercise on hold while you work on developing your emotional awareness, which is addressed in chapter 5, "Emotions." You also might want to eventually use the "Labeling Your Emotions" section of that chapter to help you identify your emotions in this exercise. (If you decide to return to this exercise after exploring chapter 5, you can remind yourself to do this by placing a sticky note in that chapter now.)

When you can reflect on your sensations—as well as all the domains of STEAM—you will be able to question your reactions to rejection. The increased self-awareness will offer you the space to consider alternatives and think about what those might feel like. All of this can lead you to develop a more positive sense of yourself, change your expectations of how others see you, and alter the course of your life.

CHAPTER 4

Thoughts

I am such a failure! I am such a failure! These words kept reverberating in Janine's head with fierce condemnation after she got fired from her job. "I had such a good future with that company," she lamented to her friend Beth, "but my boss just kept harping on me. I can't make anything work out." This opened a discussion of her mixed thoughts and feelings about herself, which went back to long before she even took the job.

When Beth cautiously reminded Janine about the good things her boss said about her, Janine bit her lip, commenting, "I know he'd compliment me at times, but that never felt as real as his criticisms." With a mix of frustration and compassion in her voice, Beth said, "You have to remember that he didn't just outright fire you. He said the job wasn't a good fit and recommended you for that other position." Janine nodded slowly as tears rolled down her cheeks. "Yeah, I know. And I know that he really does think I'd be good in the other job. I also have to admit that this job was never a good fit for me…I make it harder for myself by not believing the positive stuff. I wish I could just give myself a break."

As someone who struggles with rejection, your thoughts are very much affected by the kind of sensitivity that Janine wrestles with. You are more likely to read negative reactions from others into benign situations, or to experience situation-related rejections—such as a friend not liking your latest couch purchase—as a wholesale rejection of you. You might also be highly critical of yourself for being so flawed while continuing to try to please the other person, whom you see as more worthy than yourself. Or you might be highly critical of others, whom you are quick to see as being cruel. By focusing attention on your thinking, you can begin to see these patterns.

Like Janine, you, too, can gain some perspective on your negative thoughts about yourself or others by reflecting upon them. Your main goal of increasing self-awareness of your thoughts is not to stop your emotionally driven thinking or to start being your own cheerleader. Rather, it is to simply open yourself up to the possibility that your negative perceptions are not the accurate and full reflection of reality that you believe them to be. You may still take criticisms to heart even when you know they are inaccurate—that's okay for now. If this happens, it can help to tell yourself, "I know this is not true, but it *feels* true."

With practice, you will find that you can gain a fuller awareness of what's influencing your thoughts, the degree to which you believe them, and how they affect you. Eventually, as you increase your self-awareness in all domains of STEAM (sensations, thoughts, emotions, actions, and mentalizing), you will understand how they affect each other. To learn more about reflecting on your thoughts to develop strength and resilience, you can watch my brief video *Thoughts: Reflecting on Your Rejection Sensitive Thinking* at www.drbecker-phelps.com/home/bouncing-back/ or http://www.newharbinger.com/44024.

UNDERSTANDING EMOTIONAL THINKING

While thoughts and emotions are clearly different, that difference can be elusive. People often misuse the terms, such as when someone reflects, *I feel like I answered that question wrong.* They might mean that they think they answered incorrectly, or they feel insecure about their answer. Such confusion can make it more difficult to explore your thoughts or emotions more deeply.

So, to clarify, a thought is an idea or opinion, such as *I believe that I gave the wrong answer.* An emotion is the physical arousal you feel, along with the meaning you make from that arousal. For instance, when your heart is racing and your body is tense after you answer a teacher's question, you might be experiencing fear, or embarrassment, or both.

To complicate this situation, there is often an overlap between thoughts and emotions. Some emotions are defined, in part, by the way the person thinks. For instance, when Janine recognized how her negative thinking was hurting her, she experienced regret. In this situation, the emotion of regret includes her opinion that she was harming herself. Without that belief, she might just feel sad.

Because thoughts and feelings are so often intertwined, this chapter will often reference how feelings related to rejection affect your thinking. Also, much of this chapter offers ways for you to reconsider your emotional thinking, learning to recognize the influence of your emotions. You will be learning more about emotions in the next chapter.

Connect with Common Struggles

Rejection-sensitive people often share common themes in how they view themselves and others. This exercise will help you explore them. Grab your journal (or a pad of paper) and pencil to get started.

For the common thoughts and beliefs listed below that you most frequently experience, write down each one on the top of a separate page. Limit this to no more than three.

- I worry all the time about whether people will like me.

- I worry all the time about whether people will stop liking me and will remove themselves from my life.

- I believe others would not like me or want me around if they knew "the real me."

- If I say no to someone, they will reject me or not want me in their life.

- Other people don't want to be as close to me as I want to be to them.

- I must meet others' expectations for them to value me.

- I am not as good or worthy as other people.

- I must perform perfectly (or near perfectly) to have value or see myself as capable.

- I believe that I am basically a failure, incompetent, or lack value.

- Even when others recognize my accomplishments, I feel unworthy.

   •   If I depend on others for help, it says something bad about me.

On each page, write down examples of situations in which you had the thought that is written at the top of the page. You might be able to do this in one sitting as you reflect back on situations, but you might also find it helpful to make notes over the next few days, writing examples as they occur.

Reflect on and journal about what you've written. How does your thinking affect you? Do your self-assessments seem to be an accurate reflection of your experiences? Or do they seem more like emotional reactions?

If you have trouble separating your thinking from your emotions, consciously allow for this doubt. You may want to return to this exercise after you've explored your emotions in the next chapter. (It can even help to place a sticky note at the end of the next chapter, reminding you to return to this exercise.) You might also find it helpful to read the section, "Am I Feeling 'Rejected' or 'rejected'?," in chapter 7, "Mentalizing." You can turn to that section now, if you wish.

RECONSIDERING WHAT YOU "KNOW"

As you may have discovered in the last exercise, when you are in the grips of an emotional reaction related to experienced or feared rejection, it can be difficult—if not impossible—to think clearly. For this reason, it is important to reflect on your thinking afterward, in calmer moments. At those times, you can consider your thoughts and beliefs related to the upsetting incident. Instead of just accepting them because they feel true, you can reflect on them and even question them. You might want to journal or talk about them with a trusted person. In taking this time to reconsider your thinking, you may discover that your thinking related to rejection is biased, that what you "know" is not really true.

Your struggles with rejection can bias not only how you think about yourself but also your perceptions or assumptions about the other person. For this reason, it is important to reflect on how your rejection sensitivity might be affecting your thinking in both instances.

Explore Your Thinking

This exercise guides you in exploring your rejection-related thoughts about a situation by directing you to organize them in a chart. It focuses on your thoughts about yourself and about the person or people who you feel rejected you (or fear will reject you). You will only need your journal (or a piece of paper) and a pen. Copy the chart shown below into your journal. Be sure to use a full page so that you have enough space to fill it in. You may also use the worksheet online at www.drbecker-phelps.com/home/bouncing-back/ or http://www .newharbinger.com/44024.

Write a sentence about a situation that causes you to struggle with rejection.			
Focus	Immediate Thoughts	Reflections on Thoughts	Feelings
Me			
Others			
Situation			

Label the situation. At the top of your paper, write a sentence to explain the situation you will be reflecting upon.

Complete the "Immediate Thoughts" column. In the appropriate rows, answer the question, "What are your immediate thoughts about yourself, others, and the situation?"

Complete the "Reflection on Thoughts" column. In the appropriate rows, answer the question, "Objectively speaking, how accurate are your thoughts?" (Remember that even if they are not accurate, you might still believe them. People's beliefs are often based on their emotional experience, not their intellectual assessments.)

To help you assess the accuracy of your thoughts, you might consider these questions:

- What evidence supports these thoughts or beliefs?

- Are there times when they are not true? (Even one example of it not holding true shows that it is not absolutely true.)

- With regard to any harsh judgments about yourself or others, are there kinder ways to understand you or them that account for all of the other person's experiences or "facts"?

- Are there ways of looking at the situation that could encourage greater empathy or compassion?

People who struggle with judging themselves harshly sometimes find it helpful to consider how a good friend might think about them or how they would think about someone else in their position.

Complete the "Feelings" column. In the appropriate row, answer the question, "What am I feeling?" Consider how much your thoughts might be more a statement of how you feel than how you intellectually assess yourself, others, and your situation. If you find this difficult, fill it out the best that you can—or even leave it blank for now. You might want to return to this after you have reviewed chapter 5, "Emotions."

Completing this exercise can help you gain more perspective on your reactions. Practicing it with different situations can strengthen and reinforce this ability. Eventually, you may find that this perspective comes more quickly and easily, helping you remain calmer and respond in a healthier way to feeling disrespected, dismissed, or abandoned.

To clarify how to explore your thinking, let's look at how Robin thought about a situation she struggled with and completed this exercise.

Robin identified a situation that caused her to feel not only rejected, but also verbally attacked. She had stopped her car at a red light and then turned right into a gas station. As she pulled up to the pump, a woman stormed up and yelled at her about how it is illegal to turn right on red at that light.

After creating the chart, she followed the rest of the directions to complete it. Below are her thoughts about each question in the exercise. (You can see her completed chart online at www.drbecker-phelps.com/home/bouncing-back/ or http://www.newharbinger.com/44024.)

Immediate Thoughts: In the "Me" row, Robin wrote, "Thinking I'm a terrible driver for making that mistake." In the "Others" row, Robin noted that she viewed the woman as a crazy person, and even entertained the idea that the police should take her away. She also wrote that her boss created this problem by keeping her late and causing her to be rushed and distracted. In the "Situation" row, she wrote, "This would not have happened if there hadn't been so much traffic."

Reflection on Thoughts: Robin filled in the "Me" row by writing that she has never gotten into a car accident or gotten any tickets, so she cannot be such a bad driver. In the "Others" row, she noted that her reaction to the other woman was out of proportion and that her boss was not really to blame for the whole situation. Although Robin did not understand why the other woman was so upset, she could see that the woman was truly highly distressed. Maybe she was really upset about something totally different, but this triggered her to release that anger. Robin could relate to feeling this way. This thinking left Robin feeling curious about what could have caused such a tirade—though absolutely not accepting of the woman's behavior. Finally, in the "Situation" row, she noted that the heavy traffic was making her stressed and more likely to make a mistake.

Feelings: Reflecting on her feelings about herself, Robin wrote that she felt incompetent, inadequate, and angry with herself for this. In the "Others" row, she noted that she was afraid of the woman's anger, as well as afraid of and angry with the woman for treating her like an idiot. She was also angry with her boss for delaying her. As she wrote this, she realized that she often fears doing things wrong, leading others to dismiss and look down on her. Then when she does fall short, she is angry with herself. As she thought about her feelings in the "Situation" row, she acknowledged that she was frustrated with traffic, and this fed into her negative feelings about herself, the woman, and her boss.

YOUR PERCEPTIONS VARY BY SITUATION

Along with your sensitivity to rejection, you likely hold negative percep-tions of yourself and others. If you pay close attention, you might notice that these thoughts differ depending on the situation. For instance, you might hold more positive self-perceptions while in the company of your Aunt Jane, who has always thought you were a "beautiful angel." You might also notice that when you are with your whole family, you fear that your Aunt Jane will somehow turn judgmental (like other members of your family), even though she has always been an effective attachment figure, understanding and able to comfort you when you were upset.

Reflecting on these differences can help you be more cognizant of when you think positively about yourself and others, so that you can retain those perceptions. It can also help you remember those positives when you are thinking that there is nothing worthwhile about you, or assume that others don't want you in their life.

Note What You Are Thinking, and When

To identify and highlight when you think positively about yourself and other people, organize your thoughts in your journal.

List the main areas of your life. You might even want to subdivide those areas. For instance, you might write:

Alone time:

- Predawn yoga
- Solo lunchtime walks in the neighborhood

Personal relationships with:

- Friends: Maddy, June, Chris
- Family: Mom, Dan [brother], Uncle Bob, Aunt Wendy
- Husband
- Children

Work:

- My relationship with my boss

- My role as a supervisor

- My relationship with peers

- My skills at the paperwork part of my job

- My skills at presenting reports

Hobbies:

- Painting

For each area, make notes on how you think about yourself and others. Include contradictory thoughts. For instance, in thinking about yourself, you might write, *I usually assume people don't like me, but I also believe that my close friends like and support me. I don't question myself when I am with them.* Or, in thinking about a specific friend, you might write, *She has always been supportive, but I'm always thinking she will forget about me.*

Review everything you've written. This can help clarify areas where you have positive thoughts about yourself or others that you might normally overlook. You might also notice some themes, such as thinking positively about your competence in performing any kind of skilled activity, but questioning yourself in relationships (or the other way around).

Where once you might have fallen into the hopeless despair of "knowing" that you will be rejected forever, understanding these themes can lead you to see them with some perspective, which can be grounding.

Gaining clarity from this exercise also opens up the possibility of learning to embrace times when you hold a positive perspective of yourself or others and to respond more kindly in situations that tend to trigger your rejection-related thoughts and feelings. To help nurture the latter response, refer to the exercises in chapter 9, "Nurturing Compassionate Self-Awareness," and chapter 10, "Recovery Through Relationships."

HAS YOUR SELF-CRITICISM RUN AMOK?

If you have a sense of feeling flawed or inadequate, you may find that your self-criticism has taken on a life of its own. It stokes the fear that you deserve rejection and gives you the "foresight" to see rejection happening at every next interaction. Its powerful voice overtakes your reasoning and skews how you think. According to cognitive behavioral therapy, there are many patterns of "dysfunctional" or "faulty" thinking that create such problems for people.

Some common ones are listed below (as they relate to self-criticism and rejection). Consider whether you engage in these patterns. If you have a sense that you regularly use one or more, monitor yourself for about a week. Make brief notes each day on which type of thinking you engage in and the details of the situation. You will find that, in differing ways, they lead you to be self-critical and label yourself negatively.

The purpose of doing this is to learn to see your dysfunctional thinking. By itself, this can be a challenge. With practice, observing this thinking can help you question and eventually let go of it. Also, suggestions are offered below for what to do after being better able to identify your dysfunctional thinking.

Some common forms of dysfunctional thinking that can be damaging to you and your relationships are:

Overgeneralization: After a negative experience, you expect more of the same in similar situations. This type of thinking is marked by absolutes, such as "always," "never," "all," "none," "everyone," and "no one."

Example: After Don overhears a colleague say that he wasn't at all impressed by Don's presentation, he was sure that *no one* thought it was any good.

Mental filter: You focus on negatives about yourself, which supports your sense that you are inadequate, flawed, or worthless. You also tend not to notice or acknowledge positives. When you do notice a positive experience or feedback, you often minimize it and refocus on the negative.

Example: After being promoted at work, all Susan can think of is how she is not strong in skills needed for her new position and that she was probably only promoted because they didn't have time to find a stronger candidate.

Emotional reasoning: Your thinking is overpowered by negative feelings about yourself. This interferes with any observation, logic, or reasoning to support a more positive self-assessment.

Example: David feels so negatively about himself that he cannot believe Jen's consistently positive comments about him and their relationship. When she shows up late one night for dinner, he is immediately suspicious that she's been with someone else. His concerns are not eased even after she explains that she got held up at work on an important project he knows she's been trying to finish.

Personalization: You view yourself as responsible for problems that are not your fault.

Example: Whenever Jill's boyfriend gets angry and hits her, she frantically tries to figure out what she did so wrong. Even though she knows on another level that she doesn't deserve this reaction and that he has a history of doing this with his ex-girlfriend, she still struggles with thinking that it must be her fault.

Shoulds: You expect yourself to live up to standards that are impossible to meet consistently (if at all), and you berate yourself when you fail to do so.

Example: Rather than just thinking that he would like to do well in his classes, Andy tells himself that he has to (or should) get As. When he gets any grade less than an A, he views himself as stupid.

Catastrophizing: You perceive problems as overwhelming and catastrophic even when they are not objectively that big.

Example: During Glenn's first week as a clerk at a grocery store, his boss praised his efforts and good work ethic. But when he was late because of heavy traffic one day the following week, Glenn was sure that his boss would think he was a terrible worker and would fire him. He also imagined himself unable to find another job and that he would eventually be homeless.

If you discover that you engage in any of these dysfunctional ways of thinking, be on the lookout for them. Take note of how they increase your self-criticism, struggles with rejection, and any other consequences, such as creating a problem in a relationship. With practice, these observations will become obvious to you. The dysfunctional thoughts may begin to feel less true, allowing you to consider other ways of thinking suggested by the evidence around you.

You might also loosen the hold of your negative self-image by learning to develop empathy and compassion in relating to yourself. You will find guidance in these areas as you read chapter 8, "Building Self-Acceptance," and chapter 9, "Nurturing Compassionate Self-Awareness."

REVEALING YOUR INNER CONFLICT

When you have felt rejected, you may instinctively be defensive while also struggling with your own inadequacy. The result can be a mix of conflicted, emotionally driven thoughts. For instance, consider a situation in which a friend became upset with you for throwing her a surprise party. Part of you might have angry thoughts about how unappreciative she is. However, another part of you might feel deeply rejected by her and attack yourself for not knowing she wouldn't want the party. When such inner conflict is strong, people often feel overwhelmed and confused by their reactions.

I have frequently seen patients enter therapy because they are unhappy in their relationship, but then they talk about how things are "okay," or "not so bad." After some back and forth, we usually find that they "want" their relationship to be "fine" and appreciate many qualities in their partner, but also have serious conflicting concerns about some of the things their partner says or does. It's hard for them to address this inner conflict because they fear identifying it will lead them to confront their partner and then get rejected, or leave them with no other choice but to walk away from the relationship. When I help them understand that simply being aware does not mean they have to act in any particular way, they begin to view themselves and others more clearly and can decide how they want to proceed.

By being attuned to when you have inner conflicts, you can choose to look more closely at them. You can also pay attention to any biases you have in perceiving others, considering more consciously what might really be going on for them. When you see these different perspectives more clearly, you can weigh how each one affects you, ultimately gaining a more balanced view of the whole situation. Remember, seeing things differently does not mean you need to do anything differently. You always get to choose how to proceed. However, once people gain greater clarity about their situation, they often *want* to make changes.

Chart Your Thoughts, Emotions, and Reactions

It's often helpful to slow down your emotional thinking when you feel conflicted so that you can reflect on it. This exercise helps you do this by looking at your thoughts and emotions in a chart. Copy the chart shown below into your journal. Be sure to use a full page so that you have enough space to fill it in. (You may also use the worksheet online at www.drbecker-phelps.com/home/bouncing-back/ or http://www.newharbinger.com/44024.)

Chart Your Thoughts, Emotions, and Reactions

Conflicted Situation:		
Thoughts	Emotions	Reactions
Reflections:		

Label the top of the paper with a situation about which you feel conflicted or confused. This might be a particular event or a broader issue, such as having conflicting thoughts and feelings about your partner.

Complete the columns. Write each conflicting thought that you have about the situation on its own line. As you consider each thought, write down the emotions and reactions (in their respective columns) that seem to relate to that thought.

Review the completed chart. Once you clarify the basic conflict, you can look more closely at each of the different perspectives and consider how you might address any problems.

While you may be able to resolve some conflicts, there are others that will remain a problem. In those situations, you might need to brainstorm more about alternative ways to sufficiently (if not totally) resolve the conflict, find a way to live with it, or even leave the situation, if you can.

If you are unsure of your emotions, feel free to leave the "Emotions" column blank for now. These blank spaces can be wonderfully helpful in identifying an area of difficulty. So consider each blank space to be like a neon sign saying, "Look more closely here."

If you feel emotionally numb or are unaware of your emotions, try returning to the exercises in chapter 3, "Sensations," to help you connect with your emotions. However, if you feel your emotions but have difficulty identifying or staying with them, you might want to skip this exercise for now and return to it after reading chapter 5, "Emotions." In both situations, you might want to use a sticky note as a reminder to return to this exercise after you have completed the other work.

To clarify how to explore your conflict by charting it, consider Selena, whose youngest son just left for college. She now had to face that she felt stuck at home with her loving, yet boring, husband, Mike.

As she wrote down her thoughts in the chart, she reminded herself that while Mike was not the most adventurous person, he was open to trying new experiences when she made arrangements to do them. So, while she preferred that he initiate, she decided that she was willing to plan more activities for them, making her marriage a happier one for her (and hopefully for him, too). (You can also see her completed chart online at www.drbecker-phelps.com/home/bouncing-back/ or http://www.new harbinger.com/44024.)

Chart Your Thoughts, Emotions, and Reactions: Selena's Example

Conflict: I'm bored with my husband and my marriage.		
Thoughts	Emotions	Reactions
Husband is good man & good husband	Happy, loving	- Want to continue life together - Sometimes fear him leaving me, marriage ending
Husband is boring; just sits around	Bored, unhappy, frustrated	Want to end marriage and move on - Think of telling husband, but then fear regretting decision (remembering he's a good man); fear he would then not want to be with me and would reject me
Reflections: Mike is not the most adventurous person, but he is open to trying new experiences when I plan them. I'd prefer that he initiate, but I guess I can plan more activities for us. I think we'd both be happier.		

LOOKING BACK ON WHERE IT ALL STARTED

As you may remember from the explanation of attachment theory in chapter 1, early childhood experiences help shape the foundation of how you relate to yourself and other people (especially attachment figures). When these experiences lead you to struggle with feeling negatively about yourself or seeing others as not supportive, you are likely to be sensitive to rejection.

You may feel uncomfortable, or even fear, reflecting back on your childhood, just as many people do. They are afraid that it will confirm their worthlessness as a person or force them to remember some life-defining horrible event they previously didn't connect with their current state of distress—or possibly didn't even remember. But the truth is that what they actually learn is rarely so dramatic and is usually much more complicated.

By gaining self-awareness in all the domains of STEAM as you reflect on the possible origins of your struggles with rejection, you might find that you more deeply understand these issues. Rather than exposing reasons to condemn and reject yourself, this exploration will likely reveal a kinder, gentler, and more compassionate way of understanding yourself. As this perspective settles in, it will likely lessen the intensity of your struggles with rejection. You could then reflect more clearly on the current situation, identifying when your emotional reactions are really more about what you have learned from past experiences than they are about what's happening in the moment. This would free you to explore and enjoy relationships with people in your current life who show themselves to be trustworthy.

Use the following exercise to help you gain greater self-awareness about the possible origins of your struggles with rejection. However, if you find this emotionally overwhelming, then stop doing it for now. You might find it helpful to learn to tolerate and stay with your emotions by completing some of the sections in chapter 5, "Emotions," especially the "Sit with Your Emotions" exercise.

Think Back to Help Connect the Dots

Try to recall your earliest thoughts and emotions related to any of the following (or something else that seems similar): alone, rejected, invisible, not mattering, flawed, abandoned, inadequate, and like a loser or failure. Use these memories to complete this exercise, recording your thoughts in your journal (or elsewhere).

Answer the following questions:

- Did these memories tend to involve particular people? Who?

- If those memories occurred outside your home, do you remember having similar feelings with your parents or other family members? If so, reflect more on those memories and how those experiences affected you.

- Were there particular people who tended to respond to you in ways that left you feeling worse about yourself? Who?

- What themes do you notice (e.g., you were alone, you were being criticized, your sibling was being praised)?

After answering the above questions, reflect on them as you answer the next set of questions:

- What did these incidents teach you about your value as a person (model of self)?

- What did these incidents teach you about the possibility of others being there emotionally for you (model of others)?

- How do you think that your model of self and model of others relate to your current sensitivity to rejection?

With the insights you have gained from reflecting on the past, come back to focusing on the present. Revisit a recent incident in which you think you were particularly sensitive to being rejected or the possibility of it. If your reaction was out of proportion to that event, does your reaction fit with the childhood events that you just thought about? (Journal about this.)

In answering these questions, you might find that your seemingly irrational reactions make perfect sense when you consider the memories that they trigger.

Christine's experience in therapy is a perfect example of how these kinds of insights—and this exercise—can help. She was twenty-seven years old and came to therapy because she struggled with low self-esteem and had been feeling chronically unhappy. "I have friends," she explained, "but I'm always afraid they're going to judge me. And I never feel that they care about me as much as I care about them." Also, during the course of therapy, she began dating a man who seemed to really like her, but was similarly not sensitive to her needs. In all of these relationships, she tended to be very accommodating and did not assert her thoughts and feelings very much. Even when she did express herself, she would quickly return to being agreeable and following their lead at the first sign of disagreement.

When discussions in therapy sessions turned to her family interactions, I assigned her this exercise. In reviewing her responses, she explained, "I had always been an emotional child, something my parents couldn't relate to because they tended to be more intellectual and not particularly tuned in to feelings." She realized that they equated expressing emotions as being "bad" and (ironically) "childish."

Christine talked about how, while growing up, she had always felt undermined when she expressed herself with her parents, which—not surprisingly—she did not do often. This exercise helped her see how her tendency to remain quiet and feel "less than" carried over into her adult relationships, leading her to remain in unfulfilling relationships.

Therapy then supported her in learning more about herself, developing compassionate self-awareness (assisted by exercises offered in this book), and beginning to assert that self. In her last session, reflecting back on her growth, she explained, "I lost friendships during this process, but also found new interests and new friends." Fortunately, Christine also eventually met and married a man who respected and loved her very much.

Review Your Childhood:
A Hidden Reservoir of Strength

Even though certain childhood relationships may have initiated a critical view of yourself (along with fears of rejection), other childhood relationships may have validated a positive view of yourself (along with a feeling of worthiness). The people in these positive or healing relationships may have functioned as attachment figures that supported you through childhood and continue to bolster you throughout your life. In addition, sometimes people develop relationships in their adult lives with attachment figures who are comforting, infuse them with a positive perception of themselves, and are healing. All such positive relationships may have become inner reservoirs of strength that you already tap or that you may learn to tap.

To strengthen validating relational memories, clearly identify these relationships. Do this by asking yourself the following questions. (You may also want to journal about them.)

- Who did you turn to for comfort, support, or encouragement when you were upset or struggling as a child?

- Even when you were not upset, did you tend to feel good—and think positively—about yourself when you were with certain people? Who?

- Who have you been fortunate to have had in your adult life—even if only for a brief time—because they helped you feel comforted, supported, or encouraged?

For relationships that you found validating, ask yourself these questions:

- Given their caring responses, how do you imagine that they viewed you or still view you?

- How did you think and feel about them back then? If they are still in your life (and still supportive), how do you think and feel toward them now?

- How did you think and feel about yourself when you were with them in the past? If they are still in your life (and still supportive), how do you think and feel about yourself when you are with them now?

- Were there certain activities you did together that still feel good when you do them now (or might still feel good if you did them now)?

Sometimes people get so caught up in thinking about their struggles that they lose self-awareness for the parts of their lives that make them feel better. So, in the interest of balancing where you place your attention, use these questions to help you focus your thinking on positive or healing relationships that you have had. Also, if you hold a model of others as emotionally unavailable, this exercise might help you reconsider its accuracy in relation to past or current relationships.

To summarize, increasing self-awareness of your thoughts is not meant to turn you into an emotionless Vulcan. Instead, the idea is to introduce the awareness that your negative perceptions might not be the accurate reality that they so frequently seem to be. You may still fall into the trap of taking criticisms to heart, even when you know better. But after some practice, you can develop a fuller grasp of what influences are affecting your thoughts, the level to which you believe them, and the impact they are having on your life. As you also build self-awareness in sensations, emotions, actions, and mentalizing—the other four elements of STEAM—you can better understand how they all interact to create a richer appreciation of yourself.

CHAPTER 5

Emotions

It was a month before high school graduation. Chad looked at ease as he cruised through the party, smiling at everyone and high-fiving his buddies. But warning sirens were blaring inside his head. *Don't make a fool of yourself!* So, he was cautious about revealing much. Instead, he laughed on cue and agreed with almost everything his friends said. He repeated this agony practically every weekend through his senior year. It didn't matter that he clearly had talent as a pitcher for the varsity baseball team, that he did well in classes, or that other kids seemed to like him. *At some point, they are going to realize I'm a fake*, he often repeated to himself.

It wasn't until he was in college, listening to his friend Brett anxiously share his own fears, that Chad had a light bulb moment. *He feels just like I do!* In that instant, he was no longer alone. In seeing that Brett's fears were unnecessary, he had a sudden realization that his were, too. Afterward, he continued to worry a bit about what the guys thought of him, but he started to doubt his fear-driven thinking. With time, he was even able to sometimes calm his anxiety enough to enjoy parties and feel more comfortable with friends. Still, he was well into his twenties when he began to consciously develop his self-awareness and finally face his fears of being judged by women and authority figures.

Emotions are a part of our makeup as human beings. While you might enjoy intense positive emotions, painful or distressing ones are quite another matter. Neurologically speaking, overwhelming emotions indicate that the part of your brain called your amygdala is very active. Without getting too deeply into the actual structure of the brain, it's important to understand that when your amygdala becomes more active, your prefrontal cortex—the part of your brain responsible for thinking clearly—becomes less active. As a result, you may be unconvinced by rational explanations that "prove" you shouldn't be so upset by the idea of being dismissed or overlooked, or that might help you navigate your situation more effectively.

Because emotions are central to the richness of human experience, it is important to be able to accept all of them—the painful along with the pleasant. People with a secure attachment style can accept the full range of their emotions and are more open to life's many experiences and possibilities. They pursue love and excitedly follow their dreams. But when things don't go well, they also accept the pain of rejection or failure, and they let those feelings flow through them. As they do, they are open to the potential lessons offered by those feelings and experiences. These people tend to explore more of what the world has to offer, and they are more resilient in response to life's small and large misfortunes.

Still, their ability to experience and cope with their emotions in healthy ways can vary depending on particular situations, relationships, or periods of time in their lives.

> Teresa—who was usually resilient—felt deeply hurt and angry about being jilted by her fiancé. The emotions were so strong that she was overcome with anxiety and at times would shut down as a way to cope. This makes it hard to find a constructive way forward from the rejection. But after a time, she was able to use STEAM to calm her emotional reaction, and she became more open to seeing those feelings as an "only human" reaction that others also have. That left her more open to feeling self-compassion—to having empathy for her pain and wanting that pain to be gone. This freed her to grieve the loss and opened her to starting a new relationship.

As someone who struggles with rejection, you may find that you have trouble across situations, or your difficulties lie in one area, such as with work, friends, or your love life. But given that you are reading this book, it is taking a toll on you.

So, the focus of this chapter is to help you begin to develop a healthier relationship with your emotions by increasing an accepting awareness of them and an ability to identify them—even the painful ones. The more you can tolerate and accept your emotions (instead of trying to suppress or avoid them), the more you will be able to relate to them with self-compassion and support yourself in recovering from rejection—or at least you will be more open to nurturing self-compassion, which is addressed in a later chapter.

For those who chronically struggle with rejection, their ability to cope with it has broken down. No matter what feedback they get, they fear rejection and are constantly on alert for it. They also experience many other intense emotions. They tend to be highly self-critical, which just adds another source of rejection to their previous experience.

As with all of the domains of awareness, you will benefit from approaching your emotions with curiosity. The more you want to learn about them, the more you will get to know them and the part they play in your life. This curiosity will also help you gain more from the exercises in this chapter, which provide guidance in acknowledging and labeling your emotions. In addition, they offer a path to accepting and being more open to your emotional experiences, as well as to understanding them better. Along the way, you will find that you are less overwhelmed by struggles related to a sense of rejection.

Still, this process can be emotionally taxing. So, some of the exercises in this chapter are there to help you monitor and keep your distress within a tolerable level. You may choose to take a break from focusing on your emotions and, instead, focus on the other domains of STEAM for a while. Moving among the domains can help you explore all of them more deeply over time. (Simply use a sticky note to return to the exercises or sections of this chapter that you choose to skip over for now.)

Also, remember that thoughts and emotions sometimes overlap and almost always affect each other. To refresh your understanding of that relationship, you might review the section "Understanding Emotional Thinking" in the previous chapter.

The next section, "The Guest House," is designed to help you gain an initial understanding of how to relate in a healthy way to your emotions.

THE GUEST HOUSE

Below is a poem by Jalaluddin Rumi, a thirteenth-century Persian poet (translated by Coleman Barks). Read it. Think about it. Consider what it would be like to open yourself up to emotions in this way. (You might even want to curl up on a quiet morning or evening as you sip some tea— or wine—and savor it along with the poem.) Be prepared to reflect on any resistance you feel to doing this.

The Guest House

This being human is a guest house.
Every morning a new arrival.
A joy, a depression, a meanness,
some momentary awareness comes
as an unexpected visitor.
Welcome and entertain them all!
Even if they're a crowd of sorrows,
who violently sweep your house
empty of its furniture, **still**
treat each guest honorably.
He may be clearing you out
for some new delight.
The dark thought, the shame, the malice,
meet them at the door laughing,
and invite them in.
Be grateful for whoever comes,
because each has been sent
as a guide from beyond.

If you instinctively want to dismiss this poem and the idea of "inviting in" all emotions, resist the temptation. Instead, consciously choose to seriously consider this perspective. This might be particularly difficult for you to do with certain emotions, such as rejection, abandonment, hurt, shame, and anger. If you are critical of yourself for wanting to put distance between yourself and your emotions, imagine someone else responding in this way. You would likely understand that this other person probably wants to protect themselves against painful emotions. You might want to offer them comfort and reassurance. Practice offering yourself this same consideration.

Whatever your situation, accepting all of your emotions can open you to greater self-acceptance. You will be less likely to overreact to small rejections and more likely to tolerate any rejection. These differences in your reactions will enable you to be more resilient overall.

FACING THE DRAGON

Once upon a time, in a kingdom far away, there was a village that was terrorized by a mighty dragon. It seemed undefeatable, as there were many brave knights from kingdoms far and wide who came to slay it—only to meet their own untimely demise. One knight charged the dragon, but was flattened by the beast's enormous foot. Another met a fiery end just moments after realizing that what he thought was a mountain in front of him was actually the dragon. Years passed with many similar tales of knights attacking with all manner of weapons—battering rams, battle-axes, and crossbows. But all to no avail.

Then one day, when the village had all but given up hope, a stranger came, asking about the dragon. Unlike the young, brave knights before him, he was an older man, apparently a nomad, who had a slow gait and an easy smile. With the same quiet confidence that he had approached the villagers, he set out to meet the dragon. The villagers noted that he did not take any weapons with him—not even a sword. As he walked slowly and steadfastly up to the dragon, the great beast watched curiously. When he was close enough to touch its snout, the dragon opened its enormous mouth, inviting the stranger in. The stranger accepted this invitation by stepping inside, walking right into the belly of the dragon, and sitting down. After some angry roars and blasts of fire (which did not touch the man sitting in the beast's belly), the dragon disappeared in a puff of smoke...leaving the tranquil stranger in peace.

Your emotions—especially those related to rejection—can be frightening "beasts" that can feel powerful enough to incinerate you. But, in fact, their great strength is magnified by your reaction to them. When you learn to approach your emotions with calm acceptance, you limit their power.

I imagine you might have two pressing questions in reading this: *Is it really humanly possible to feel calm in the face of your emotions?* And, *If it is, how does that disempower them?*

Let's start with the second question. While your emotions are automatic reactions to triggers, they are also the result of many factors, which continue to influence your emotions for as long as you feel them. Your emotional reaction may be unduly influenced by recent or long-past experiences, or in response to faulty suppositions about yourself or others. Also, the unknown can instill fear, which can further fuel your emotional reactivity. So, the more you understand yourself and your emotional reaction, the less it happens *to* you, and the more you can influence the experience.

As for the question of whether you can learn to face your emotions with relative calm, the answer is that you absolutely can. It will take some learning and practice, but you can gain the skills and experience to face your emotions with curiosity, rather than just enacting them or trying to avoid them.

As you will learn from this chapter, there are many ways to explore your emotions and get to know them better. From your first efforts forward, one of the best "tools" is your curiosity. Wonder about your emotions. With each exercise, be curious about how they can help you. This by itself can reduce the apprehension you may feel in exploring your often emotionally intense inner world.

Because the journey can be intense, it is important that you learn to pace yourself, testing your limits but not pushing too hard. The next section—"Visualizing a Safe Experience"—is aimed at helping you learn to calm yourself when you feel hurt, ashamed, dismissed, or generally upset. This can enable you to continue moving forward when you might otherwise be too overwhelmed to do so. Then there are exercises designed to help you experience and understand your emotions. As you get more comfortable with your emotions, you'll find that you also achieve greater self-acceptance, enabling you to have greater self-compassion.

Overall, you will gain more clarity about yourself and your situations, moving you toward having healthier responses, including reducing your oversensitivity to rejection and feeling better able to cope with it when it does happen.

VISUALIZING A SAFE EXPERIENCE

Recovering from rejection requires that you feel emotionally safe enough to let go of trying to prevent rejection at all costs, or to allow for feeling it when it happens, rather than defending against it. This can open a door to your inner world. Then, in getting to know yourself better and to engage more completely in your experiences, you can learn to participate more fully in relationships despite the possibility of further rejection.

This process isn't about someone "making" you feel safe. It's about you finding safety within yourself, though often with the support of others. One way that sometimes helps people feel safe is to think about a place (real or imagined) that they find calming and comforting. You can also find a sense of safety through the caring of people in your life. But when you do, it is because you have let in that caring. So, you can also access the comfort and support of relationships by thinking about them. Together, feeling safer with yourself and with significant others, you can enjoy more securely attached relationships that are not weighed down by chronic feelings of rejection.

When deciding on a safe experience, there are no limitations on what setting might be helpful. Many people choose settings in nature, such as the woods or the beach. You might choose your home or the home of your childhood. You can also choose outer space, deep under the sea, or what you imagine heaven looks like. If you choose to reflect on a safe relationship with an attachment figure you can turn to for comfort, it can be with a loved one, a religious figure, a fictitious character, or even your pet (yes, Fido qualifies). But whatever you pick, your goal is for the setting and supportive figure to be comforting ones.

Plan for some undisturbed time to practice this visualization. Do your best to engage all of your senses. Imagine the sights, sounds, and physical sensations of being in your safe place or with your safe figure. The imagery might even include your sense of taste. The more real you make it, the more calming the experience.

Practice imagining this experience during calm times until you can do it with relative ease. Then choose to go there whenever you are overwhelmed by feelings of rejection (or any other emotions). But rather than using it as an escape, choose to use it as a way to help you feel stronger as you work through a difficult situation, enabling you to face feelings of rejection as they happen. Or, if that is too difficult, you can use this strategy to "step back" from the situation and help calm you. Then reengage in addressing the situation at a later time.

LABELING YOUR EMOTIONS

Remember the neurological explanation in the beginning of this chapter of how emotions can deactivate your clear-thinking prefrontal cortex? Even as your brain is responding this way to your emotions, you won't necessarily realize it. Although you might feel intensely emotional, you might also not be aware of your emotions—or only have a vague sense that they are there. For instance, your annoyance with a coworker who seems to be avoiding you may be the only sign of a volcano of anger within you (in response to the avoidance) that's simmering underneath. This is an example of what might be an unconscious attempt to dismiss the importance of feeling rejected by others. But it's a way of coping with rejection that can often backfire.

Alternatively, you might be acutely aware of your reaction to feeling rejected. Janine had been aware of struggling with this and with feeling negatively about herself ever since she was young, when her mother was extremely critical of her. In her current life, she easily feels dismissed by people, which elicits intense feelings. She is sometimes so hurt or afraid that she feels like she is emotionally imploding. Unable to think clearly or calm herself, what could Janine do?

If only she could deactivate her amygdala—turning it off with the flip of a switch—she would feel calmer and perhaps think clearly. Though your brain doesn't exactly have such a switch, scientists have found something that can sometimes work like one—or at least like a dimmer switch. Identifying and labeling your emotions can energize your prefrontal cortex, which is associated with decreasing activity in your amygdala. Put more simply, when you label your emotions, you often feel less emotionally reactive. Importantly, you can still acknowledge and feel your emotions, but they don't overwhelm you or your thinking.

Given that identifying your emotions is a skill, you must make a conscious effort to improve it. Find time to sit down, connect with what you are feeling, and then label your emotions. When you find yourself trying to understand or rationalize them away, choose to redirect yourself to simply observing and labeling them.

You might find it helpful to begin by focusing on your emotions when they are less intense—such as when you begin to feel concerned about someone not returning your calls. As your skill in labeling your emotions grows, you will find that you are better able to do it when you are more upset. (If you have trouble recognizing your emotions before they are intense, read the upcoming section of this chapter called "Observing the Intensity of Your Emotions," along with the associated exercise, "Rate the Intensity of Your Emotions.")

It's not uncommon for people to have difficulty labeling their emotions, especially when those emotions are strong. One way to help yourself with this is to refer to the List of Emotions on page 193; it is also online at www.drbecker-phelps.com/home/bouncing-back/ or http://www .newharbinger.com/44024. Some people find it helpful to keep the list handy so that they can check it when they are confused or emotionally overwhelmed. (You can download it and carry it with you.)

If you cannot label your emotions because you have trouble physically connecting with them, try doing the "Reconnect with Your Senses" exercise in the chapter 3, "Sensations."

If you can physically connect with your emotions and label them, the next step is to allow yourself to spend time with them. To learn more about this, see the next section, along with the associated exercise.

THE IMPORTANCE OF CONNECTING WITH YOUR EMOTIONS

Too often, when Janine's rejection sensitivity was triggered, she avoided her emotions by putting extra effort into taking care of other people, eliciting positive feedback from them, and easing her fears of rejection. But after she practiced sitting with her emotions, she was able to stay with them more, which gave her the opportunity to process those emotions (reducing their intensity), let go, and move on.

Opening yourself to your emotions begins with choosing to give them your attention. If you have no idea what you are feeling or even whether you are feeling anything, you might find it helpful to begin connecting with your emotions through your body. To do this, complete or revisit the exercise in the "Reconnect with Your Senses" exercise in chapter 3, "Sensations," and then return to this exercise.

Sit with Your Emotions

Once you are able to connect with your emotions, this exercise directs you in how to spend some quiet time with them. Although there is no standard amount of time for this exercise, make sure you will not be disturbed for at least 10 minutes. (You can increase your time with practice.)

Allow yourself to be aware of your emotions. They might be mild, barely worth your attention—but attend to them anyway. Or they might feel powerful. Take the time to identify each emotion and let yourself really feel it. This part of the exercise can, by itself, be difficult.

When you feel a number of emotions, single out one that is particularly intense or important. For instance, if a disagreement with a friend recently turned nasty, you might be powerfully afraid of her never talking to you again. But you can choose to focus on your sense of annoyance, which is comparatively weak. Though you may be unsure why you made the choice, you might still have a sense that it was important.

Whatever emotion you pick, attend to it without trying to change it. As you stay with it, you might notice that it changes on its own. That's okay. Perhaps that mild annoyance with your friend grows to being "peeved" and then angry. Next, you might feel afraid of your anger—more specifically, you might feel the fear of rejection that has seemed to haunt you forever. In this way, the unfolding of your emotions increases your self-awareness and can even offer great insight. So, just keep paying attention until you feel that your work is done for the time being.

When you find that you get distracted while sitting with your emotions, remind yourself to refocus on them. You might need to do this several times. Many people also find it helpful to bring their attention back to their bodies and then notice that particular emotions arise from their bodily sensations.

Identifying and feeling your emotions is a process and an end in itself. So, don't try to rush through it. Be patient. You may find that you remain somewhat confused even when you finish. That's okay. This is an exercise to be repeated, and your emotions will reveal themselves in time.

OBSERVING THE INTENSITY OF YOUR EMOTIONS

As you pay closer attention to your emotional experiences, you can learn to distinguish how each emotion changes as it increases or decreases in intensity. This increased awareness is an important part of getting to know yourself better and can transform your emotions or enable you to manage them better. For example, consider this story:

> Soon after Chad and Linda began dating, Chad's thoughts kept returning to the fear, *Is she going to leave me?* While he was passionately in love with her, the slightest action on her part— such as getting momentarily distracted when they spoke—could send him deep into an emotional abyss of feeling rejected. From out of nowhere, his positive and negative emotions seemed to overwhelm and control him. But that changed when he learned to pay closer attention to the weak signals of his emotions and to increases in their intensity. He learned to rate the intensity of his emotions "Happy" and "Afraid" along scales, as shown in Figure 5.1.

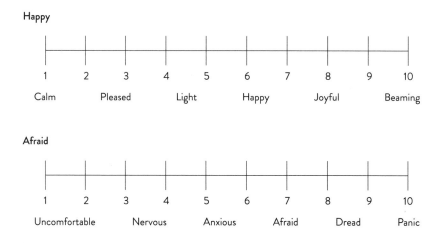

Figure 5.1   Chad's Scales of Emotional Intensity: Happy and Afraid

Not surprisingly, he liked practicing attending to the "Happy" scale and rating the intensity of that feeling. He was aware that he would sometimes feel calmed from being with Linda (rated 1 on the "Happy" scale). With more attention, it would sometimes morph into him smiling with happiness (rated 6), whistling joyfully (rated 8), or even what he called beaming with delight (rated 10). He noticed that doing this helped him more fully appreciate, and sometimes even extend, those feelings. However, he also noticed that the feelings would often drop as his levels on the "Afraid" scale increased.

As Chad practiced attending to his fear, he learned to rate the intensity of it, noting that he was first aware of feeling uncomfortable, which was a 1 on the "Afraid" scale. It would then increase to being fidgety and anxious (rated 5). As it increased, he felt a bit shaky and afraid (rated 6), and then he began sweating and could feel his heart pounding as he was overwhelmed with a dread of her leaving him (rated 8 or 9).

Along with rating his emotions, he learned to respond differently to them. Rather than just passively feeling the tightening grip of his increasing fear, he practiced becoming curious about whatever intensity of emotion he was experiencing. At first, he would just bring his awareness to the feeling and stay with that. Often, this alone eased the intensity.

When it didn't—or didn't ease it enough—he wondered about the feeling. *What was making him feel this way? Was it really in response to what Linda was doing, or more about what he thought she might do? Did he really have reason to expect she was going to leave him?* (He learned to steer away from focusing on the future, which tended to increase his fear and distress.)

In addition, attending to the intensity of his fear of rejection taught him that no matter how intense his fear became, it always faded with time. From this, he realized that his feelings of rejection have a "life cycle." So, when his fear of rejection became overwhelmingly strong, he could remind himself of the common phrase, "This too shall pass."

You can learn more about connecting with your emotions by watching my brief video *Emotions: Opening to Your Rejection Sensitivity* at www .drbecker-phelps.com/home/bouncing-back/ or http://www.newharbinger .com/44024.

Rate the Intensity of Your Emotions

To help increase your awareness of the intensity of your emotions, this exercise will guide you in creating and using a scale of an emotion. You might pick fear, anger, or another emotion. Similarly to Chad, you can choose to create more than one scale, though you might want to start with just one.

Copy the scale below. Assign a word to describe how you feel at different levels of intensity. While you do not need to label all ten levels, be sure to label several of them.

1   2   3   4   5   6   7   8   9   10

Use the scale to identify when the intensity of your emotion impairs your thinking. When you reflect on increasing levels of the emotion, you will notice that there comes a point when you begin having difficulty thinking clearly. (This can happen even with pleasant feelings, such as when people who are in love ignore signs of their partner cheating.) Circle the number that best represents that level of intensity.

While creating your scale(s) can increase your awareness of your emotions, you can also use the scale(s) to practice being conscious of the increasing intensity of your emotions in your daily life.

Regularly practice being conscious of the levels of intensity leading up to the number at which you have trouble thinking clearly. As your emotion approaches and exceeds the number you circled, you will find it increasingly difficult to tolerate or manage that emotion or to think clearly. The more you practice rating your emotions, the better you will be at tolerating and regulating them. That will make them less likely to spiral out of control.

Even as you become more adept at rating your emotions, you may still struggle with being overcome by them. As you approach your circled number, you might try using the "Sit with Your Emotions" exercise earlier in this chapter. If your emotion is too intense for you to "sit" with, you might want to use some of the suggestions offered in the "Learning to Self-Soothe" section in chapter 2. Also, some of the sections in chapter 3 might help, such as the "Mindful Breathing Meditation" and "Walking Meditation" sections. Once you feel less overwhelmed by your emotion, you can return to attending to it and its many levels.

MAPPING YOUR JOURNEY OF EMOTIONS

Certain situations can cause you to immediately feel intense rejection and anxiety, just as facing a tiger might trigger panic in you. However, learning that the tiger is actually behind thick glass will likely have a calming effect on you. Similarly, gaining greater self-awareness about your emotions can help you reflect upon them and develop a greater sense of calm. You will still feel emotions in reaction to events in your life, but you may suffer less—and you may become more open to enjoyable feelings.

Dr. Paul Ekman, a pioneer in the research of emotions, joined with the 14th Dalai Lama (spiritual leader of Tibet) to create a map (or an atlas) of emotions, which you can see at www.atlasofemotions.org. The website helps people understand how they experience and process what he defines as the five universal emotions: anger, fear, sadness, disgust, and enjoyment.

To help you understand this model of emotions better, consider the diagrams that are presented in Figure 5.2 of each of the five universal emotions as they might be experienced by rejection-sensitive people. (These diagrams of emotions can also be found at www.drbecker-phelps .com/home/bouncing-back/ or http://www.newharbinger.com/44024.) Based on a modification of Ekman's timeline of emotions, they show how sensations, emotional thoughts, and emotions influence behavioral reactions. I specify thoughts as "emotional thoughts" because they are a way of thinking that is strongly influenced by emotions.

Using this model, you can gain a better understanding of how your struggles with rejection play out. Based on life experiences and your sensitivity to rejection, you may feel fear of rejection even when a friend or partner is simply offering a suggestion, such as for improving communication between you by asking you to lower your voice. As you can see in the "Fear" diagram in Figure 5.2, your fear might be accompanied by sensations of rapid heartbeat, sweating, and nausea. It might also be accompanied by emotional thoughts of assuming the other person will be critical of you, seeing you as somehow unworthy or unlovable, and possibly abandoning you (physically or emotionally). Your behavioral reaction might be to become extremely agreeable in the moment and perhaps follow up by frequently texting or calling.

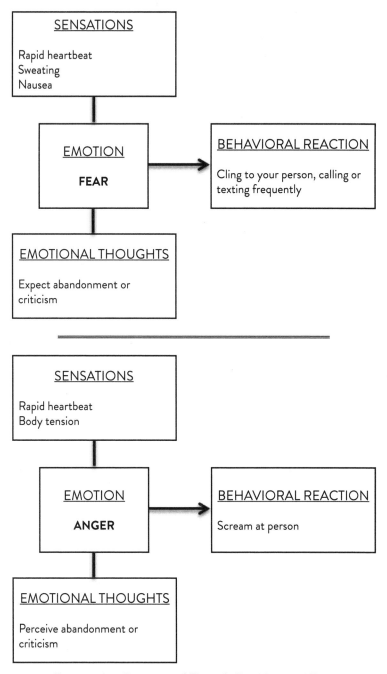

Figure 5.2 Diagrams of Ekman's Five Universal Emotions, as rejection-sensitive people might experience them (based on Paul Ekman's timeline of emotions, found on www.atlasofemotions.org)

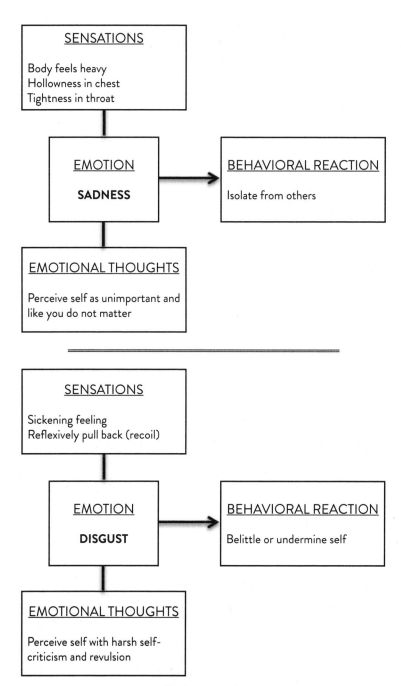

Figure 5.2 (cont.)

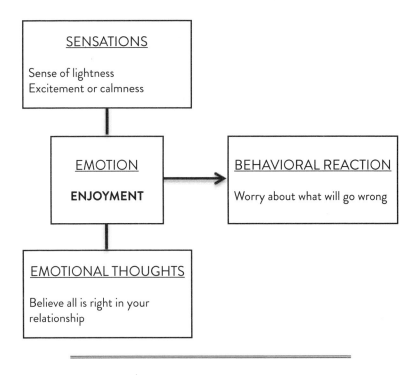

Figure 5.2 (cont.)

Increasing self-awareness of emotions can help you *consciously respond* rather than just *automatically react* to circumstances. Although this chapter is focused on your emotions, you can learn to help yourself by intervening at any of the domains of STEAM.

Follow Your Emotional Process

After reviewing the diagrams in Figure 5.2, think about a situation in which you struggled with rejection. Then grab your journal (or a piece of paper) and a pen to complete this exercise. Copy the chart shown in Figure 5.3 on a page of your journal. You may also use the worksheet online at www.drbecker-phelps.com /home/bouncing-back/ or http://www.newharbinger.com/44024.

Complete the "Emotion" box with a specific emotion. You may feel many emotions in response to struggling with rejection, but choose just one for the purpose of this exercise.

Complete the "Sensations" box. Take a deep breath and pay attention to your body. You may find it helpful to close your eyes. Some people also find it helpful to slowly scan their body from their feet up to the top of their head. Doing whatever works for you, observe any notable sensations, and then write them in the appropriate box.

Complete the "Emotional Thoughts" box. Reflect on the chosen situation and pay attention to your thinking. Write down your thoughts related to rejection in the appropriate box.

Complete the "Behavioral Reaction" box. Thinking back on the situation, observe how you acted in response to it and write this in the "Behavioral Reaction" box.

After completing the whole diagram, review it. Allow yourself to become more conscious of all the factors at play in this emotional situation. This awareness may, by itself, help you respond differently in future emotional situations. Also, you might find it helpful to repeat this process for other emotions in the situation you just reflected on or for other situations.

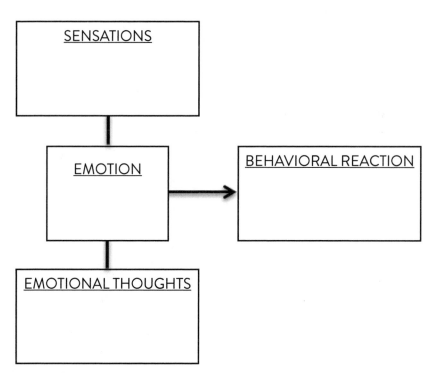

Figure 5.3   Follow Your Emotional Process

If you think that your sensations, thoughts, or (re)actions are causing you greater difficulty with your emotions, you might want to turn to those particular chapters to learn how to address those domains.

LIGHTENING YOUR LOAD ONE EMOTION AT A TIME

Being rejected can feel like an explosion that sets off an emotional land-slide. In the end, you might feel like a boulder has landed on your chest, making it hard to get up and move on with your life. But if you pay closer attention, you'll probably find that there's not a single boulder there. Instead, it's a pile of rocks. This is an extremely important difference. Although you probably would not be able to move a huge boulder off your chest, you would be able to lift one rock at a time and move it aside—eventually allowing you to get free. And that's kind of how it works with emotions.

An undifferentiated combination of many intense emotions might be overwhelming and confusing, and feel like an all-encompassing mass of anxiety. It is too much to take on at once. However, an awareness of the many emotions in that massive experience, such as fear, hurt, and sadness, might be more manageable. For this reason, it's important to identify the different emotions that make up your "boulder" and then address them one at a time.

Accomplishing this task is a bit complicated, but you can do it by focusing on one step at a time. You will be returning to some of the exer-cises presented earlier in the book. Read through this section to learn which exercises are needed to help in this task. If you have not already worked through any of the exercises, go back and complete them one at a time (rather than trying to learn them and put them together in one sitting).

Begin the Offloading Process

Once you have worked through the earlier exercises and are ready to use them here, set aside some uninterrupted quiet time in a comforting place. You will need enough time to settle down in a comfortable chair, separate out your emotions, and regroup before moving on with your day. I suggest beginning with at least 20 minutes.

Attend to your emotions. If you have difficulty focusing immediately on your emotions, you might begin with the "Reconnect with Your Senses" exercise in chapter 3, "Sensations."

Identify the emotions. Label the emotions you are feeling. (If you need help with this, review the "Labeling Your Emotions" section earlier in this chapter.)

Focus on one emotion. As you become aware of the emotions stirring within you, choose to focus on one. Do not try to do anything with the emotion other than keep your awareness on it.

Complete the "Sit with Your Emotions" exercise. If you do not remember this exercise from earlier in this chapter, review it before just trying to stay with your emotion.

After completing this exercise, you will probably still feel quite emotional. However, you will be better able to process your emotions and consciously take steps toward recovering from rejection.

You may want to repeat these steps for other emotions, though I don't suggest you do this all in one session. It takes time and can be emotionally draining. You will most likely need to go through this exercise many times to identify and experience each significant emotion that is part of the "massive boulder" pinning you down. But each time you do, you will likely find that your experience becomes clearer and less overwhelming.

IDENTIFYING LEVELS OF EMOTION

Understanding your inner emotional landscape is particularly complicated because you not only have emotional reactions directly to situations, but you also have emotional reactions to your emotions and thoughts. Emotion-focused therapy identifies these two levels of emotions as primary and secondary emotions (Greenberg, 2010).

Primary emotions are your initial reactions to a situation. You might feel happy, sad, hurt, afraid, ashamed, or lonely. They are an expression of your authentic or "true" self.

Secondary emotions are your reactions to your initial thoughts and emotions—not to the situation. For instance, you might feel frustrated or angry with yourself for feeling hurt (and in your assessment, weak). You might also be angry with yourself for feeling hopeful that things can get better because you believe that it only sets you up for more rejection.

Secondary emotions "protect" you from connecting with your primary emotions, which can seem too threatening or painful, but they do this at a price. For example, you feel frustrated or angry with yourself (secondary emotions) for feeling hurt (primary emotion) by the dismissive comment of a friend. Then your angry, self-critical thoughts may grow. As long as you are engaged with them, you will not be consciously feeling the pain of rejection or may have hope to avoid feeling that way again—but you will also be perpetuating a negative view of yourself.

To further elaborate on primary emotions, some people get stuck in maladaptive ones, such as being prone to responding to even the slightest rejection, or the possibility of rejection, with intense fear, anger, or sadness. When you recognize this maladaptive pattern, *do not* try to force yourself to feel differently or even berate yourself for feeling as you do. Instead, with the emotional distance you might feel in watching a character in a movie, simply notice how your response is disproportional.

To free yourself from the emotional mire caused by rejection, it is essential that you bring your awareness to these primary and secondary emotions. Get to know them. After some self-exploration, you might observe that becoming more aware of your hurt (primary emotion) causes you to reflexively revert back to your anger (secondary emotion). This observation is key in helping to change, because it offers a pathway back to your primary emotions. Continue to observe this.

There is no doubt that our emotions are deeply rooted, inextricably intertwined with the other domains of STEAM, and complicated to understand. However, they add richness to what would otherwise be drab and unfulfilling lives. So, as you learn to open to your emotions—especially those tied to your feelings and fears of rejection—without being a prisoner of them, you will feel set free. You will learn to enjoy a life where you embrace your inner self and can take the risk of sharing that self with significant others.

CHAPTER 6

Actions

"Fine!" Janine yelled into the phone as she stabbed at the red "end" button. *If she's really my friend, Gina will apologize,* Janine muttered to herself. She tried to get back to writing her daily to-do list, but she kept glancing at her phone, unable to concentrate. Then it occurred to her; she was the one rejecting Gina, not the other way around. Gina wasn't urging Janine to stand up for herself as a way to put her down or be mean. It was because Gina cared about her. Although Gina *had* hurt her feelings, she had also apologized for that. If only Janine had really been listening to Gina, she would have heard the concern in Gina's voice. Then she would have felt cared about instead of attacked. After chewing on this—and the end of her pen—for a while, she took a deep breath and picked up her phone. "I'm sorry..."

Your actions express your sensitivity to rejection and perpetuate it in ways that you may not even be conscious of. Developing a fuller awareness of your actions opens you to an opportunity for greater self-understanding through them and the other dimensions of STEAM. You can then acknowledge and "own" your experiences and behaviors.

This is what happened for Janine, who realized, after some reflection, that she had hung up on Gina based on emotionally influenced thinking, not the reality of the situation. With her change in perspective, she felt differently about the interaction, prompting her to reach back out to Gina. Similarly, you will find that greater awareness of your actions will lead to a change in your relationships with yourself and others.

This chapter explores gaining greater awareness of your actions from observing verbal and nonverbal communication in any given conversation, as well as in patterns you repeat over time. For example, your sense of feeling unworthy may express itself in your slumped posture, as well as in the way you repeatedly put yourself down. Sometimes such patterns of behavior elicit criticism from friends or family—which only serves to reinforce your negativity toward yourself. When you can consciously see these dynamics, you have the chance to pause and think about them, enabling you to better understand yourself and others. As a result, you are more likely to feel greater empathy for yourself, opening you to feeling greater compassion. From this new perspective of compassionate self-awareness, you can choose to act differently.

This chapter also encourages you to be more aware of how activities affect you. Your insights can help you choose to engage in ones that facilitate growing and healing. It addresses how mindful actions can help you stay in the moment rather than getting swept away by your fears and feelings of rejection. And it addresses how, when you are discouraged, you can work to appreciate a comforting touch from people who care about you. Learning to take this in can help you turn to them (as an attachment figure) for reassurance when you feel upset. In addition, you can supplement the skills offered in this chapter with those in the "Learning to Self-Soothe" section of chapter 2, such as by practicing yoga or doing a craft. By adopting these many ways of actively coping when you feel rejected, you can ease your distress, think more clearly about the situation, and respond to rejection with greater resilience—all of which will help you become more securely attached and less sensitive to rejection.

In addition to the information presented in this chapter, you can learn more about the importance of attending to your actions in my brief video *Attending to How Rejection Affects Your Actions* at www.drbecker -phelps.com/home/bouncing-back/ or http://www.newharbinger.com /44024.

UNDERSTANDING NONVERBAL COMMUNICATION

Messages communicated with the wholeness of someone's being have more weight than those communicated with dry words. These messages are delivered with many actions, such as facial expressions, gestures, and behaviors. Nonverbal communications (and their meanings) often happen outside of people's conscious awareness, which can make them even more impactful. With your sensitivity to rejection, you are likely to erroneously experience other people's nonverbal cues as powerfully rejecting and to unconsciously express your struggles in a way that perpetuates them. But when you begin to consciously pay attention to these communications, you can learn to recognize them, clarify their messages, and reconsider your response to them.

With this in mind, review the following kinds of nonverbal communications. Then, when you observe examples of them in your daily life, consider what they might be saying—and what you might be misinterpreting.

Prosody: This is the pattern and rhythm of speech, such as the volume, pitch, and tempo. It also includes the emotional tone, such as being gentle, happy, excited, strident, condescending, sarcastic, or threatening. These cues suggest the emotional state of the speaker and indicate their thinking and the next actions they might take. Depending upon your perception of prosody, the same words, such as, "Yeah, I love you" can be a source of comfort or a trigger for being consumed by a sense of rejection.

Posture: When people stand in an upright posture with shoulders back, they are physically grounded and stable in their bodies. It tends to communicate self-assurance. However, when the body is held rigidly and movements are not smooth, a person can appear highly anxious. You might notice that your torso tends to slouch when you feel dismissed or defeated. Sometimes when people notice someone else has good posture, they become more self-conscious and feel more inadequate, perhaps even imagining that they are being judged.

Body placement: If you are dating someone who stands and sits close to you, they are likely showing romantic interest. On the other hand, if they give you plenty of personal space, that distance may indicate that they do not currently want greater closeness. However, to guard against misinterpretation, it is essential that you stay as close to the facts as you can while interpreting the meaning of a person's body placement.

When Linda remained a bit physically distant from Chad on their first date, he fell headlong into rejection and despair. However, this reaction was premature. As he later found out, she liked him, but needed some time to get comfortable.

Physical reactions: Many involuntary physical reactions can be observed. People's faces often turn red when they are embarrassed or angry. Their bodies sometimes shake when they are afraid. And their breathing is often constrained when they are anxious and fearful of rejection.

Gestures: People often communicate with gestures rather than words, such as when someone waves you to come closer. However, as with verbal communication, you must understand gestures in their context.

Eye contact: Maintaining eye contact is often used to intensify an experience. When people feel loving, holding eye contact expresses greater emotional closeness. However, when linked with being angry or judgmental, it can be threatening. By contrast, avoiding eye contact generally increases distance or lessens emotional intensity. People may avoid eye contact when they are lying or when they are uncomfortable with closeness for other reasons, such as fear of being judged.

As you attend to nonverbal communication, you may gain insights about yourself and other people. But beware of your bias to see rejection where it does not exist, or to perceive it as bigger than it is. Be sure to double-check your interpretation of nonverbal messages with other information, such as the context of the situation and the nature of the person you are interacting with.

BURNING YOURSELF OUT

Sometimes it may seem like you are a perpetual motion machine in taking care of life's to-do list, but you also feel like you are just doing what's necessary. Anything less and other people will have no use for you. Still, you have to admit that it takes a lot of effort. You might even feel like there is something wrong with you for having to work so hard.

Some downsides to your massive efforts—to your almost constant busyness and actions—are that you seem to always feel deeply unfulfilled, at the end of your rope, or like you have no gas in your tank. But slowing down might not feel like an option. You may fear that this would only reveal your flawed self to everyone…and that would lead to the unacceptable fate of them dismissing, abandoning, or rejecting you. Yet, continuing at your current pace feels impossibly draining.

If you are nodding as you read this, then it is extremely important that you understand: Life does not need to be this way. There are people who do their best, take care of themselves, and have a positive self-image, despite not being the best at something or not meeting their own or others' expectations. Not only are these people often outwardly successful, but they also feel good as a person even when other people don't like them, are critical of them, or outright reject them.

With this in mind, reflect on your efforts to perform well and their effects on you.

Are You Doing Too Much?

To determine whether you are working too hard, choose a situation in which you think you are acting in an extreme way, such as regularly working 70 hours a week or never saying no to a friend's requests. Then, do the following:

Make a pros and cons list. The pros side of your list might include that you feel like a good friend or you are excited about advancing at work. On the cons side, you might note that you have no time for friends or activities that you enjoy. For people who stay motivated through self-criticism, the cons list will also include things like continual self-doubt and general unhappiness despite any successes.

Reflect on your list. Ask yourself, "Does this ultimately make me happy or feel fulfilled?" If you accept that you are making sacrifices now for the future, consider whether there will really be a time when your actions will lead to a sense of success and fulfillment. If you realize that you are not happy and expect that you will forever be chasing approval, be clear with yourself that your excessive efforts are not working well, even if you are outwardly succeeding in the moment.

Consider an alternative approach in which you accept your needs and your limits. Imagine choosing a more balanced life. Fears of failure and rejection will undoubtedly arise. As they do, challenge the criticism that probably accompanies them. For example, question whether you would really think less of a colleague or friend who led a more balanced life.

(If you see yourself as not just busy, but as a perfectionist, this will be addressed in detail in the chapter 7 section "When Perfectionism Falls Short" and the related exercises.)

If you can see how your fears of rejection lead to your excessive busyness, but can't seem to change it yet, that's okay. Remember, this is just one step toward your goal of overcoming your sensitivity to rejection.

You may want to pay daily attention to how your excessive efforts are related to your self-criticism, fear of rejection, and unhappiness. Consider what your reaction might be to others whom you respect, but are not so perfect. You might also find it helpful to keep a diary of these observations and thoughts.

PROTESTING REJECTION

Janine is constantly fearful of not being good enough, and therefore being rejected by friends. She *protests* this by frequently texting or calling them. She also fills her days with helping them with anything and everything. While she enjoys being helpful, she is also unconsciously driven to make herself indispensable.

Many people sense that they cannot expect to be loved for who they are, but rather need to earn the acceptance and caring of others. So, when they feel that they have been dismissed or abandoned—especially by attachment figures—they often respond with protests like Janine's, pushing back against the rejection or trying to earn (or earn back) approval.

Some of the many actions people take to protest rejection and try to gain other people's approval are:

- Requesting practical help and emotional support

- Caretaking

- Remaining almost constantly connected with people in person, on the phone, or through social media

- Being highly physically affectionate, such as with hugging, kissing, and being physically intimate

- Using deceit and manipulation to keep people personally engaged

At other times, they engage the anger they feel by:

- Expressing hostility (This can be both an honest expression of anger and an "opportunity" for others to show caring by trying to appease them.)

- Being passive-aggressive (For instance, while Janine feared that expressing her anger toward friends for perceived rejections would lead to even more rejection, she would often not return their texts or calls.)

Paying attention to your protests against rejection will likely make you more conscious of your feelings of rejection, in addition to the other domains of STEAM. As you become more self-aware, you can practice reflecting on how you want to respond to these experiences rather than reflexively reacting. For instance, aware of your inclination toward care-taking, you might be conscious of how you immediately insist that your friend choose the restaurant when the two of you plan to go out to dinner. You might also notice that you are suddenly disconnected from any sensations of hunger—an experience that you know is related to sublimating your own needs.

In addition to becoming more aware of your actions and related experiences, you might reconsider your perceptions of the other person. Let's say that you tell your friend who prefers barbecue that you want to eat Chinese food. Now you fear your friend is frustrated. Even if that is true, contrary to how it feels, maybe they still like and accept you as a whole person. Or perhaps they are not upset with you at all. Instead, they might be distracted or upset with something having nothing to do with you.

With a greater appreciation of the needs underlying your protests, you will be more inclined to respect them. You will have a conscious choice for new ways of acting that you never had before: attend to the other person's needs, advocate for yourself, or find a way to balance both.

LEARNING TO RESPOND CONSTRUCTIVELY

By reflecting more on your actions and reactions, as well as your *possible* actions and reactions, you can begin to consider the consequences of them. Then, when faced with a situation, you will be more likely to respond thoughtfully rather than just reflexively reacting.

As mentioned in chapter 5, Dr. Paul Ekman is a pioneer in the research of emotions. He created a map (or an atlas) of emotions, which you can see on www.atlasofemotions.org. On this website, he illustrates that people can have three categories of reactions to their emotions: constructive, destructive, and ambiguous.

To understand these reactions, note how Janine moved between all three of them in this situation:

> When Janine walked into the yoga studio, she immediately approached Beth, who was talking with a new woman. "Hi, Janine. This is Pat," Beth said, offering a broad smile, but then immediately turning back to Pat. Janine's heart beat quickly as she irrationally imagined Beth turning her back on Janine and befriending this new woman. She felt like she didn't matter and was almost immediately overwhelmed by feelings of rejection. At first, Janine pretended to be lost in thought, not being bothered (an ambiguous reaction). Later, she "joked" about Pat's matronly appearance (destructive reaction). This annoyed Beth, creating the very distance that Janine feared. However, when Beth was late to the next class, Janine talked with Pat alone. As it turned out, despite her reservations, she realized that she liked Pat and chose to engage fully in the conversation (constructive reaction), which eventually grew into a close friendship.

To clarify these three categories of reactions, review Figure 6.1. (These diagrams of emotions can also be found at www.drbecker-phelps .com/home/bouncing-back/ or http://www.newharbinger.com/44024.) You may recognize that the diagrams in this figure are very similar to those in the "Mapping Your Journey of Emotions" section of chapter 5, "Emotions." However, in this section, the diagrams are expanded to illustrate the three options for reacting to the five universal emotions that Ekman has identified—fear, anger, sadness, disgust, and enjoyment.

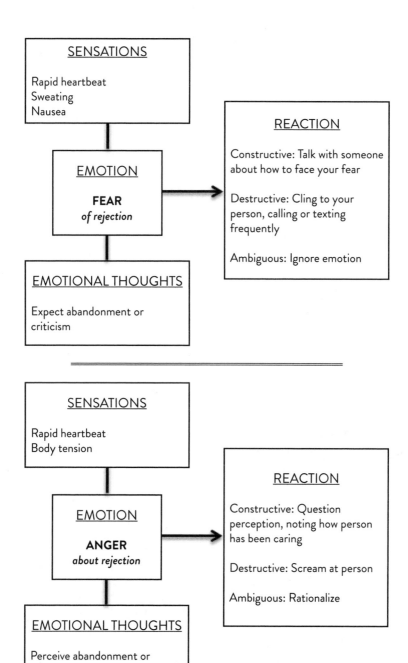

Figure 6.1 Diagrams of Emotions with Constructive, Destructive, and Ambiguous Responses (based on Paul Ekman's timeline of emotions, found on www.atlasofemotions.org)

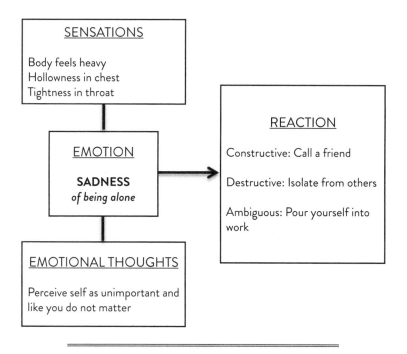

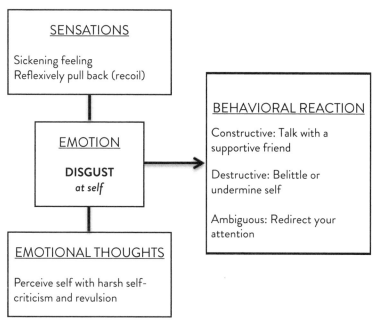

Figure 6.1 (cont.)

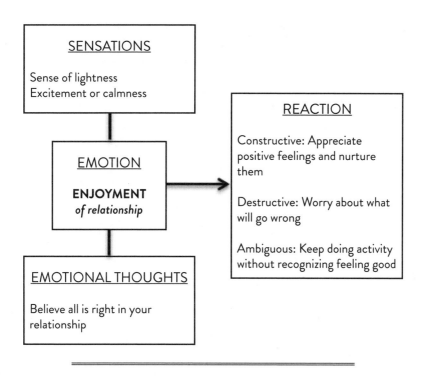

Figure 6.1   (cont.)

Observe Your Responses and Consider Your Options

This exercise is designed to help you recognize your own automatic reaction to rejection and to consider various possible responses. However, because it builds on the "Follow Your Emotional Process" exercise in chapter 5, complete that exercise before doing this one. You will need your journal (or a piece of paper) and a pencil to complete this exercise.

Think about a situation in which you struggled with rejection.

Identify the emotions you felt. They may or may not include Ekman's universal emotions.

For each emotion, copy and complete the chart shown in Figure 6.2 on a page of your journal. You may also use the worksheet online at www.drbecker-phelps.com/

home/bouncing-back/ or http://www.newharbinger.com/44024. Be sure to place your reaction next to the appropriate label of constructive, destructive, or ambiguous. Circle this reaction. Next, fill in possible actions for the other two labels.

You might notice that your reaction in a given situation is constructive. Still, fill in the destructive and ambiguous reactions. You might recognize these as reactions you have had in other circumstances. By completing all of the reactions in the diagrams, you are enriching your understanding of the various ways you can respond to your emotions, along with clarifying which ones are the most constructive.

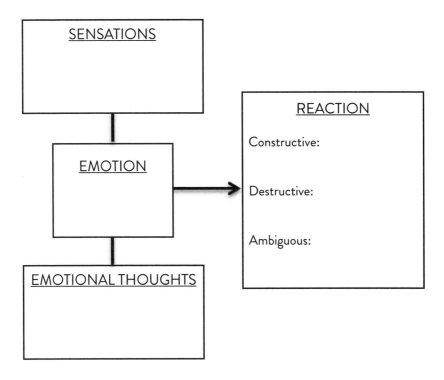

Figure 6.2   Observe Your Responses and Consider Your Options (based on Paul Ekman's timeline of emotions, found on www.atlasofemotions.org)

If you want, you can extend this exercise by completing another diagram for your emotional responses to your reactions. For instance, if your emotion was sadness and your reaction was emotional withdrawal, you might notice that this reaction caused despair. You might also note that a constructive response would be to call a friend, who could help you feel comforted. Next, you could extend the exercise by completing diagrams for the emotions of despair and feeling comforted. This process of following your emotions, the different aspects of them, and your reactions to them can enable you to have greater personal insights that lead you to choose healthier reactions.

KEEPING BUSY: DISTRACTION VERSUS FULFILLMENT

> Chad couldn't take it anymore. Why hadn't Linda called him this morning like she usually did? *I must have done something to turn her off...but what?* He didn't dare call her, or she would surely tell him their relationship was over. Of course, he knew this was crazy. *We had a great time last night at the movies and dinner. And I'm sure nothing could have changed since then,* he puzzled. But all the logic in the world didn't change the sickening feeling he had inside. So, he needed to get busy doing something, anything, to distract himself.

My patients often tell me how their emotional pain can overtake them, and that they cope by doing things to keep their minds off of their thoughts and feelings of rejection. But when we look more closely at the things they do, it becomes apparent that not all activities are the same. While some behaviors are purely distractions, others offer more personal fulfillment.

Purely distracting activities take your mind away from your struggles with rejection, though they do not inherently nurture your inner self. You might play games on your phone or get lost in mind-numbing Internet surfing. Whether the distractions are fun or neutral, their main importance is that they allow you time to calm down. But for them to be helpful in the long run—as opposed to just a momentary escape—you must reflect on your struggles once you feel calmer. It is most effective to return to the topic when you still feel somewhat emotional about it—albeit not when you are overwhelmed. While it can help to reflect much later when the feelings are "cold," that's not as effective in helping you manage your emotions.

Though pure distractions have their place, engaging in personally fulfilling activities can nurture a sense of self-worth while also distracting you from distressing situations. Of course, just as with purely distracting activities, it is important to reflect back on your struggles with rejection after you feel a bit calmer.

> Chad had noticed that when he became a paramedic, he felt better about himself, because he was part of a team that was serving the community. On the morning when Linda didn't call him, someone called to ask if he would take their shift. While he continued to worry about his relationship, the work definitely redirected his attention *and* gave him a sense of value and fulfillment. Then when he returned home later, he had the emotional strength to text Linda. By then, he could see that he had overreacted. That's when he learned that she had slept all day because she was feeling sick.

You can build meaningful or fulfilling activities into various aspects of your life, such as:

Work: learning new skills

Hobbies: completing a family genealogy, designing homemade birthday cards

Religion: praying, being part of a social-action committee

Volunteer: fostering animals

Family: spending the day with a sibling and their family

Social life: going to a concert or having a barbecue with friends

The more you can connect with inherently having value and feeling fulfilled, the stronger you will feel in facing your fears of rejection. Rather than feeling like you are being rejected as a whole person, you might realize that someone is taking issue with some aspect of you, such as your sense of humor or your politics. You might also recognize that you are simultaneously being accepted and valued in another situation or another relationship (as Chad did with his paramedic work). Although these differing experiences can be confusing at first, the practice of observing these different aspects of your experiences will help you gain a sense that rejection is not all-encompassing.

By using your "go-to" fulfilling and distracting activities when you are upset, you can help yourself calm down, think more clearly, gain a greater sense of having value, and even feel less overwhelmed with rejection.

(For more on developing a positive sense of yourself, turn to chapter 8, "Building Self-Acceptance," and chapter 9, "Nurturing Compassionate Self-Awareness.")

ACTING MINDFULLY

Your feelings of rejection can prompt you to think and feel particular ways that then lead to other painful thoughts and feelings, and this chain reaction can continue on. Very soon, you are likely no longer acting in response to the reality of a situation, but are instead going in circles or spinning off into the netherworld of internally created struggles. For instance, you may be snapping at a friend who stood you up, before you even register that she is telling you she got in a car accident. And it began with wandering off in your own head, rather than remaining connected to the moment.

To help keep you closer to the current circumstance and to the actual actions of others (rather than your fear of what they are doing or might do), it is helpful to have reminders to stay present—or be mindful—built into your day. Some people do this with rituals, such as saying grace before they eat or, for Jews, touching a mezuzah before entering a home or room. A less inherently meaningful, yet potentially powerful, way to develop the ability of being mindfully present is to choose an action you perform regularly.

When I am in my office, I have practiced being more fully aware of the moment as I touch my doorknob to open the door for my next patient. You might choose each time you pick up your phone or stand from your chair. You might also choose more extended actions, such as walking more slowly and mindfully from your car to your office each day, or taking a shower with more mindful awareness. The options are limitless.

> Aware that his mind often wandered off, Chad decided to practice a mindfulness exercise. He chose to attend to the experience of chopping a carrot while he cooked dinner. As he picked up the carrot and placed it on the cutting board, he noted its temperature and texture. He was even aware of its smell. Then, as he picked up the knife, he brought his attention to its weight and the texture of the handle. He slowly chopped the carrot, being aware of the changing sensations in his hand and arm as he did so. He also noticed and appreciated his wonderfully designed and functional hand as he chopped vegetables for his meals.

Whenever you perform a mindful action, do so slowly and with more focused attention. It's okay when (*not if*) you find yourself doing these actions mindlessly. The idea is not to perfect being focused, but rather to help yourself live more mindfully even as you continue to get pulled back into old habits, daydreaming, and mindless action. That's why practitioners of mindfulness call it a practice.

COMFORTING TOUCH IN YOUR RELATIONSHIPS

> Whenever Janine's "touchy" friend Beth hugs and kisses her on the cheek, she can feel her body stiffen. As she became conscious of this, she began to wonder about her reaction. Although she was hungry for approval, she was uncomfortable with physical

affection. *Beth has always been a caring and dependable friend*, she thought. Then she reassured herself, *Hugging and kissing are Beth's way of showing she cares about me*. Janine decided to work on being more open to Beth's physical affection. When Beth hugged her, she took a slow, deep breath, and consciously relaxed her muscles. She paid attention to the warmth she felt in her body and noted, *I can feel her caring*. It took a number of times doing this before Janine was able to feel positively about it—even if she was still a bit uncomfortable.

Comforting touch (such as a hug or feeling a hand on your shoulder) can trigger the production of oxytocin, a hormone that can bring down stress hormones and, in turn, bring on a sense of trust, safety, and connection. Oxytocin can have such a powerful effect that it has been dubbed the "cuddle hormone." Once released, it can help you feel emotionally safer, allowing you to be more aware of your emotions, able to tolerate them better, and even share them with others when you might otherwise suppress them. When—through repeated interactions—you associate someone with this sense of comfort, you are likely to see them as a possible source of soothing when you are upset (making them an attachment figure).

Along with these benefits, the act of someone touching you can also increase your sense of vulnerability, and so you might reflexively steel against the comforting effects of touch. If you struggle with this, respect your innate need to protect yourself. Rather than trying to force yourself to accept physical comfort, be curious about your defensive wall and consider what it might be like to let it down a bit.

If you can relate to Janine's discomfort and are open to trying to change this, consider your relationships carefully. Is there someone whom you believe that you can trust and feel safe with? If so, you might want to practice being more physically expressive, such as by hugging to say hello or goodbye. If you think it would help, ask for their support in this. Another option is to get professional massages. Or you can get creative, such as joining a ballroom dance class. (Note: People with a history of abuse often find physical closeness very challenging and should not force themselves to engage physically with other people. Instead, it is important for them to nurture self-compassion—as addressed later in this book—and perhaps work with a therapist on their struggles.)

Keep in mind that when you touch others, their oxytocin levels will probably increase, so they'll be more likely to return the favor. For instance, as Janine became more open to Beth's hugs and kisses, she even initiated a hug one day when Beth was upset, which made Beth visibly happier. Of course, you must gauge how open the other person is to being touched by you, and specifically to the way in which you touch them.

Increasing touch can reduce the intensity of your distress enough that you can tolerate it better. In doing so, you might find that you can think more clearly about your struggles and even be more understanding and responsive to others—such as when Janine was able to be aware of Beth's need for comfort and to offer it.

Open Yourself to Hugs and Emotional Closeness

One way to become more aware of how open or closed you are to being comforted is to pay attention to your experience when hugging, or accepting a hug from, someone you love. This could be a partner, friend, or family member. To help you with this, complete the following very brief questionnaire in your journal (or on a piece of paper) and consider what your responses mean.

Think about your general experience when you and someone you love are hugging. Write down your rating for each statement on a scale of 1 to 5, with 1 being not at all and 5 being very much. Then add up your ratings for a total.

- I sense caring *from* the other person.

- I feel caring *for* the other person.

- I feel emotionally comforted by the hug.

- The hug helps physically calm my body.

Consider what your total rating means, and journal about it. Understanding that the lowest total score you can get is 4; the lower your score is, the less open you are to absorbing the love offered. If certain scores are higher or lower than the rest, think about what that is saying about you and your openness to physical affection and emotional acceptance. For instance, you might rate the statements about being comforted or calmed by a hug lower than the other statements, reflecting a difficulty in emotionally taking in a hug despite registering it as a message of caring.

Consider, and make notes about, whether you would respond differently to different people. If you would, look for themes. For instance, some people are very open to receiving physical comfort from women but not men, or from children but not adults.

Open your mind to, and write about, the implications of this exercise. Think about how your openness to physical affection influences your sense of feeling cared about or feeling alone in the world. Reflect on the different themes that you notice. Consider your thoughts related to the physical experience of hugging.

These observations and insights can enrich your understanding of yourself. That is important, even if nothing changes immediately, because it can eventually lead to being more open to letting down that defense.

After completing this exercise, when someone hugs you, consciously choose to be open to the caring they are offering, as well as the physical warmth. If you try to take in a hug but don't feel comforted, it's okay. That's your starting point. You can just continue to be aware of your experiences when you hug. Feeling the warmth may come with time and with the other inner work that you are doing.

By becoming more aware of your actions, the messages that they communicate, and how they relate to the other domains of STEAM, you will understand yourself better. You can then choose how you want to act, rather than reacting reflexively. This might mean learning new coping behaviors so that you can feel emotionally stronger and be more resilient to rejection. It might mean choosing an "appropriate" response when you recognize your emotional reactions as being out of proportion to the situation. Or it might mean using your developing self-awareness to increase empathy with your struggles with rejection. As you continue reading this book, you will learn to use that empathy to develop greater self-compassion, which will then enable you to be more resilient to rejection.

CHAPTER 7

Mentalizing

"I'm going to need to stay longer than I thought," Linda said solemnly, as she explained that her mother was having more problems from her stroke than they originally thought. Chad's heart immediately began pounding hard, the way he imagined it would if it received an electric jolt by one of those defibrillator paddles.

As Linda explained more, he realized that he wasn't following a word of what she was saying. Aware that he was not there for her as she had been there for him these last two years, he forced himself to focus. He consciously attended to the *sensation* of muscle tension in his chest, *thoughts* that she was abandoning him, *emotions* of feeling rejected, and *action* of not saying a word. That's when he realized that his old abandonment fears had overtaken him. Fortunately, he was then able to refocus and be supportive of Linda rather than spiraling into his own personal crisis.

When Chad used his deepening self-awareness through STEAM to understand his own and Linda's responses, he was *mentalizing*. This means he could "get" where she was coming from when she decided to stay longer with her mother. It also means that he could "get" *himself*, and that his initial reaction was motived by old abandonment fears. Experts sometimes refer to mentalizing as "holding the heart and mind in heart and mind." That is, you recognize someone's thoughts and feelings (their "heart and mind") with both an intellectual understanding and an emotional connection to their experience (your "heart and mind"). You can do this when relating to other people, as well as to yourself.

While it might sound confusing, mentalizing is something you do every day without even thinking, such as when you hold the door for someone entering a store behind you. But when you become emotional or feel strain in a relationship, it helps to be more conscious of your mentalizing (technically called "controlled mentalizing"). When Chad consciously mentalized by making himself aware that Linda was really acting out of concern for her mother (not a desire to distance herself from him), he was able to respond with caring rather than react with anger or hurt. Chad's experience shows how consciously mentalizing is very helpful in clarifying misunderstandings.

Importantly, mentalization is not solely an intellectual process, such as when a movie critic coldly picks apart why characters behave a certain way. This would be called "pseudo-mentalizing" because it is done while being emotionally disengaged. Instead, your heart and mind both need to be engaged to fully appreciate someone's experiences in this way.

The better you are at mentalizing, the more you can understand yourself and others. In addition, it can help you tolerate, and feel less distressed by, your emotions. This allows for greater empathy, compassion, and ability to truly forgive. For example, if a coworker expressed their frustration with you for interrupting their work, a weak mentalizing ability would leave you feeling like their response was an indictment of you as a whole person. On the other hand, a strong mentalizing ability would allow you to understand that they were expressing a momentary feeling. You could empathize with what it feels like to be interrupted when you are highly stressed and focused on a task. By improving your mentalizing ability, you will also think more clearly and flexibly—which would include being more resilient in the face of small and large rejections. You can learn more about using mentalizing to address your struggles by watching my brief video *Mentalizing: A Way of Overcoming Rejection Sensitivity* at www.drbecker-phelps.com/home/bouncing-back/ or http://www.newhar binger.com/44024.

To complete the exercises in this chapter, it is important that you have worked on developing all of the other domains of self-awareness. By having an awareness of your sensations, thoughts, emotions, and actions, you can consciously challenge your tendency to automatically become overwhelmed by rejection or any experience even slightly resembling rejection.

USING ENGAGED CURIOSITY WITH YOURSELF

Remember *Curious George*? That little monkey was lovable because of his playful nature. His natural sense of wonder led him to explore the world with an openness to learning. This same curiosity and openness to learning can help you increase your self-awareness.

But the quality of that curiosity is extremely important. You can have nonjudgmental curiosity—which I call *engaged curiosity*—or judgmental curiosity, which I call *critical curiosity*. When applied inwardly, *engaged curiosity* opens you to new experiences and can help you understand yourself better. For instance, in thinking about wanting to make your living as an artist, you might muse, "I wonder what it would be like to be a professional painter?" By contrast, you might be *critically curious* and, in the tone of an inquisition, ask, "What do you want to do *that* for?" In response, you would likely feel criticized, and so you might shut down your self-awareness. When this happens, you become more of a stranger to yourself, and your ability to mentalize inwardly becomes impaired. By contrast, practicing engaged curiosity encourages you to be more open with yourself. You feel accepted and have a sense of safety that allows you to lower your defenses, be more self-aware, and mentalize yourself better.

Learn to Develop Engaged Curiosity

You can further develop engaged curiosity by completing this thought experiment:

Reflect on a time when you felt rejected. Replay it in your mind well enough to connect with your thoughts and feelings at that time.

Be curious about your reaction. Ask yourself, "What was going on for me?" Access the other domains of self-awareness in STEAM. If you are unable to connect with experiences in a particular domain, use some of the exercises in the chapter for that domain. This will help you gain a full understanding of your experiences and elicit empathy for them.

Consider other reactions that people might have to this circumstance. It might help to think of how particular people you know might react differently. Maybe they would feel rebuffed, but not deeply hurt. Or maybe they would not feel rejected at all. They might also feel disrespected or angry.

Reflect on what might be causing your reaction. Rather than letting yourself just slip into familiar old reactions, use your awareness of other possible reactions to try to understand what is causing you to respond in this way. You might consider how the current circumstance would make most people feel at least somewhat rejected. You might also note how certain aspects of the situation remind you of other, deeply upsetting situations. Or the fear of not being good enough might be related to a deeper fear that has been with you since childhood—an issue that might need to be explored further to more fully understand.

Affirm your understanding. Once you "get" why you responded as you did, it is important to realize that your reaction is a human one. Given your particular circumstance, you would likely feel empathy for someone else having the same reaction. Allow yourself to have empathy for it...and for yourself.

Think about doing this exercise as a way to practice engaged curiosity, as you would do for any new skill. If you realize that you have returned to old patterns, simply acknowledge it, along with how difficult it is to develop this skill. You might take a breath and try again, or give yourself a break and return to practice this exercise at a later time.

As you strengthen your ability to use engaged curiosity, it can help you cope better in the moment when you are feeling dismissed or rejected, or to recover more quickly afterward. To be curious in this openly engaged way, you must think about yourself from a caring—or at least nonjudgmental—perspective. If you are unable to do this even when you are in a positive frame of mind, turn to chapter 8, "Building Self-Acceptance." Take some time to work on feeling more positively toward yourself. When you are better able to think of yourself in an open and positive way, return to this exercise. (You might want to place a sticky note in chapter 8 to remind you to return to here when you feel ready.)

USING ENGAGED CURIOSITY WITH OTHERS

It is just as important to approach others with engaged curiosity as it is to approach yourself with it. When you do, you will feel more open to what the other person is expressing, enabling you to have empathy, understand them better, and nurture the relationship. And when you feel increased trust, you are more likely to feel safe turning to them for comfort at times when you are upset and vulnerable (seeing them as an attachment figure), and not be as likely to fear or feel rejection. As the relationship strengthens to become more securely attached, it may support you in feeling better about yourself.

One way to nurture engaged curiosity with others is by picking a friend or family member with whom you feel relatively safe. As you talk with them at a time when you don't feel tension between you, listen for a topic where they struggle emotionally. Ask questions that help you connect and have empathy for their experience. Even if you feel a strong desire to help them, choose to stay focused on really "getting" what they are going through (you can problem solve later). If they feel understood and cared about, they will probably share more and eventually feel the intensity of their emotions lessen. Once you have developed this skill when you feel safe, strengthen your ability by practicing it when you disagree or feel upset with the person.

Another way to nurture engaged curiosity is to pay attention when you assume someone's ambiguous behavior is expressing a critical view of you. Just as many people find that increased self-awareness opens them to engaged curiosity, Janine also discovered this for herself:

> *Oh, no. Here we go again,* Janine thought. She was sure that Gina was distracted because Janine bored her. But then she had a flash of awareness for how she often overreacts. So, instead of letting that sick, nauseated swirl of rejection pull her under, she chose to pause and think. *OK, maybe she is tired of me, but maybe there's a different problem. Maybe work has finally gotten to her. Or maybe she's gotten more bad news about her mother's health.*
>
> As Janine reflected on the possibilities, it occurred to her that she really did not know what was going on—and that it made no sense to assume Gina was done with her. Still unsure, she was at least able to keep a more open mind. *I really wish I knew what was going on,* she thought. And then, almost without realizing it, she asked, "You seem distracted or upset. Do you want to talk about what's going on?" That simple question

opened the floodgates, with Gina pouring out many struggles she had kept inside.

By thinking about another person's inner experiences, you are practicing mentalizing that person. Although you can only ever guess at someone else's inner experience, mentalizing them can help you better understand their actions and be more open to cues that belie that experience. As a result, you can connect better and have healthier, happier relationships with less fear of rejection.

ASSESSING YOUR CURRENT SITUATION

When you are having an emotional reaction out of proportion to a situation, it is natural to wonder what is going on. Rather than starting with deep psychological issues, begin more simply. Consider current unrelated factors that might be affecting you.

For instance, if you feel terribly hurt in response to a generally supportive friend gently teasing you about getting lost driving to meet her, understanding your struggles with rejection can make sense of your reaction. However, another helpful insight might be that you ate two doughnuts for breakfast and are likely experiencing a plummet in your blood sugar levels.

So, before you explore the depths of your psyche for why you are overreacting, ask yourself these questions:

Is there something going on with me physically? Some examples are:

- Hunger
- Tiredness
- Pain
- Illness
- Drunkeness

Am I upset with or about someone else? Some examples are:

- Parent

- Friend

- Child

- Partner

- Coworker

Did one or more situations happen recently that have affected my mood? Some examples are:

- Recent problems at work

- Financial difficulties

- Car accident

If you do identify external stressors, then it is important to consider how strong an effect they are having. This will open many choices of how to respond. You might want to turn your attention from your current reaction—such as feeling hurt about being teased—and focus on one or more of these problems. You might tell the person you are upset about these other factors, or you might remove yourself from the situation and handle the other issues separately.

Be sure to consider whether the problem is a chronic one that requires attention. For instance, if you regularly eat doughnuts for breakfast, switching to a healthier alternative could work wonders. A few common examples are in the following chart. If you struggle with other problems, add them to the list, along with their solutions. Then make a plan to take action on the proposed solutions for your problems, creating healthier habits.

Problem	Solution
Tired	Get rest. *Chronic:* Take action to increase your regular sleep or address insomnia.
Hungry	Eat a balanced meal or snack. *Chronic:* Develop a plan for healthy eating, including a balanced diet with appropriate portion sizes and eating at regular intervals.
Illness	Get rest and take medicine as needed. *Chronic:* Consult with a doctor and follow through with recommendations.
Angry with a particular friend	Address the issue with your friend. *Chronic:* Reassess that relationship and how you want to deal with ongoing issues.
Financial difficulties	Develop a plan for addressing the problem. *Chronic:* Reassess your way of managing finances.
Feeling burned out from life stressors	Do activities that nurture yourself, such as taking a hot bath or giving yourself permission to have a fun, stress-free day. *Chronic:* Build activities into your regular routine that can help give you the strength to continue on. Reconsider your priorities.

Finally, if a current stressor or difficulty seems to be causing ongoing strain and you have been unable to adequately address it, seek professional help.

AM I OVERLY SENSITIVE TO REJECTION?

After their most recent argument, Chad feared Linda would leave, which shook him to his core. It was like an inner earthquake that set off a tsunami of emotions. He was repeatedly slammed by powerful waves of self-loathing and anger with Linda. *She can be such a bitch*, he growled to himself as he got more caught up in how she didn't care and how she had ruthlessly hurt him. Any sense of emotional stability he felt was undermined by a growing conviction that all people are cold and heartless, even though many pretend to be nice.

These thoughts felt real to Chad despite evidence to the contrary. When someone responds in an overly sensitive way to rejection, they are react-ing—overreacting, really–with a sense of being Rejected (with a capital R). By contrast, when they react to rejection in a way that is more in proportion to a situation, they are responding to it with a sense of being rejected (with a lowercase r). This is the difference between Chad feeling Linda simply wasn't being fair versus feeling cruelly rejected by her.

So, while Chad had friends and family who often called him out of concern, he still experienced himself as all alone in the world. He was unable to hold his negative thoughts and painful feelings back—much as no one can hold back tidal waves. Though he felt like this crisis would never end, his intense emotions eventually calmed on their own. His emotionally driven thoughts continued to exist, but he held them less intensely, and they were not as central in his conscious thoughts.

As Chad discovered, when you recognize you are experiencing Rejection, the ability to calm your emotions enough to think more clearly is essential. People can often help calm themselves in various ways, such as the activities described in the "Learning to Self-Soothe" section of chapter 2. That section includes many suggestions for self-soothing and describes some techniques for relaxing. If you do not have activities that you can rely on to help you feel better and you are frequently overcome with anxiety or distress, you might review that section now.

As you feel less overwhelmed, you will likely gain some perspective. You might recognize that it looks from the outside like you are "making a mountain out of a molehill." But this probably won't feel true. In fact, you might be deeply, painfully hurt when a coworker doesn't think to invite you to lunch, or when your spouse says that she would like to spend some time alone on the weekend. Despite your objective thoughts, your sense of rejection feels more real.

The truth of the matter may be that your reaction is out of proportion to the *current* situation. However, the very real pain is telling you that there is more to the story. As I explained in chapter 1, it can help to think of your emotional sensitivity to rejection as similar to the sensitivity that a burn might cause to your skin. In both cases, even a gentle touch to that sensitive area (skin or sense of rejection) can feel unbearable because of previous experiences.

Once you can recognize that you are having a sense of being Rejected (with a capital *R*) rather than rejected (with a lowercase *r*), you can begin to question it. It's important not to question the validity of your feelings, because they are neither right nor wrong—they just exist. Rather, your feelings can be in keeping with a situation or misaligned with it. So, you might say to yourself something like, "I'm feeling Rejected with a capital *R*." That statement can be a signal for you to think more about what might be triggering the feeling. If it does not seem to fit the current situation, it comes from past experiences. This awareness can help move you toward being less sensitive to real or potential rejection, dropping unnecessary defenses, and ultimately opening up to feeling closer with others.

Consider whether you become so overwhelmed by "Rejection" that it is difficult for you to reflect on the feeling. If it is, then you may find it helpful to complete the "Sit with Your Emotions" exercise in chapter 5. When you are able to "sit with" your emotions, then you might explore the origin of your feelings by completing the "Think Back to Help Connect the Dots" exercise in chapter 4.

WHEN PERFECTIONISM FALLS SHORT

One way people try to avoid rejection is by being "perfect." After all, if you get everything right, you have shown that you have value to yourself and others. But perfection—or excelling beyond reasonable expectations—cannot be maintained, and there is always the threat of falling short. So, moments of feeling "good enough" tend not to last long. Even at the height of your success, you may continue to feel below the surface that you are only successful because you have tried so hard, or were lucky. You believe that you don't really deserve—and won't be able to continue—being successful and valued. These thoughts, not surprisingly, can leave you feeling depressed and anxious.

You may intellectually know upon reflection that you are not a loser or failure. You may know that there are people in your life who truly care about you. Unfortunately, "knowing" the truth won't automatically help when the negative and self-critical thoughts "feel true." But with this intellectual awareness, you can question your "felt truth." Rather than attacking yourself for your perceived failures and "deserved" rejection, you can choose to be deeply curious about what is going on within you.

A good way to start is to clarify whether (and to what extent) you engage in two kinds of perfectionism: self-evaluative perfectionism and socially prescribed perfectionism (Reis and Grenyer 2002).

> James is near the top of his class in medical school. Unrelentingly self-critical, he gripes to himself, *I might as well be at the bottom of my class.* True to his nature, instead of feeling proud of his accomplishments, he remains steadfastly focused on being at the top of his class. He is driven by a sense he'd always had that he needed to be ahead of the pack in order to be okay or have any value.

Similar to James, you might not consciously worry much about what others think of you. Instead, you might use self-evaluative perfectionism to focus on personally defined high standards—maybe even unrealistically high ones. By meeting those standards, or at least surpassing other people's accomplishments, you sense that you can prove to yourself (and others) that you have value.

Rate Your Self-Evaluative Perfectionism

The following sentences are thoughts that reflect self-evaluative perfectionism. In your journal (or on a separate piece of paper), rate how much you relate with each statement on a scale of 1 to 5, with 1 being not at all and 5 being very much. Then add up your ratings to find your total score.

- It's very important to me to strive to be as perfect as possible in completing tasks.

- I feel driven to keep working on a task until it is perfect.

- I set very high expectations for myself.

- I am rarely, if ever, proud of my accomplishments.

- When I have attained a goal, I immediately focus on the next goal without much appreciation for what I have achieved.

- Even when there are objective signs of success (e.g., recognized by a boss, earned an award, hired for a job), I continue to be self-critical or focus on what I have not achieved.

Understanding that the highest score you can get is a 30, the higher your score, the more that you value yourself based on meeting unrealistically high standards.

Consider and journal about the meaning of your score. As your score approaches 30, consider how your perfectionistic tendencies might be backfiring. Rather than helping you feel accomplished and secure in your value, they might ultimately be reinforcing your sense of not being good enough. Even when you are successful, it may never feel good enough, prompting you to forever be pursuing the next goal so that you can feel okay about yourself.

Reflect more deeply on your self-evaluative perfectionism. Though it takes courage, choose to focus on all the domains of awareness in STEAM as they relate to your perfectionism. When you need help with a particular domain, use the exercises in the chapter on that domain to help you. For example, use the "Reconnect with Your Senses" exercise in chapter 3 to tap into your physical sensations as you have these perfectionistic thoughts. Engage in the "Sit with Your Emotions" exercise in chapter 5 to allow yourself to become more aware of the emotions related to your perfectionism. And use the "Are You Doing Too Much?" exercise in chapter 6 to see how your efforts to be perfect affect you. While exploring and reflecting on your perfectionism in the domains of STEAM, journal about your thoughts and insights.

As you develop a fuller sense and appreciation of your self-evaluative perfectionism, you will find that you begin to question it, and perhaps consider healthier ways of relating to yourself.

As you get to understand yourself better, you may look upon yourself with greater acceptance and compassion. You will not be as self-rejecting, or expect others to be as rejecting, if you fail to live up to your high standards. To whatever degree you see this progress—or even if you don't see it much at all yet—that's okay. These patterns are often very entrenched. Keep your struggles with self-evaluative perfectionism in mind as you read chapter 8, "Building Self-Acceptance," and chapter 9, "Nurturing Compassionate Self-Awareness."

> Not thinking about what she needed to do to take care of her own three children, Nancy thought, *Rhonda's job is crazy busy this week, so she could really use a hand.* She immediately found a way to cook dinners for Rhonda's family, chauffeur her kids, and be there to listen to Rhonda's frustrated rants about her supervisor. There's nothing wrong—and a lot that is right—with all of that…except that Nancy was muttering angrily to herself for having less to give to her own family and work. In other words, it was so important for her to be a good friend to Rhonda that she didn't take into account her own needs.

Similarly to Nancy, you might engage in socially prescribed perfectionism, focused wholeheartedly on perfectly meeting or exceeding your perception of other people's standards. If you excel in what others are looking for, then they won't reject you—or, at least, that's how this thinking goes. If you are the nicest person possible, or the best worker your boss has ever seen, you will likely get positive feedback that can help counter your sense of lacking value. The problem is that the sense of being essentially flawed will still be there, needing to constantly be proven wrong. This can produce chronic and even disabling anxiety.

Because Nancy had been increasing her self-awareness of STEAM, she realized something was not right about her response. Then she thought about how she was always totally there for her friends—much more than they were there for her, and more than she would expect anyone to be there for her. She also realized that while she liked being helpful, she feared that others would not want to be her friend unless she made herself irreplaceable.

Rate Your Socially Prescribed Perfectionism

The following sentences are thoughts that reflect socially prescribed perfectionism. In your journal (or on a separate piece of paper), rate how much you relate with each statement on a scale of 1 to 5, with 1 being not at all and 5 being very much. Then add up your ratings to find your total score.

- It is extremely important to me not to let others down.

- I often feel anxious at the thought of disappointing people.

- Most people I know are disappointed in me when I make mistakes or fail at a task.

- I try to avoid making mistakes so that other people don't get upset with me.

- When I make mistakes or fail at a task, I feel like this shows I am not as good as other people.

- I often fall short of meeting other people's expectations of me.

Understanding that the highest score you can get is a 30, the higher your score, the more that you look to others to assure you that you have value.

Consider and journal about the meaning of your score. As your score approaches 30, it reveals a great tendency toward unhealthy attempts to perfectly meet or exceed what you think others would want from you. Think about how this tendency is affecting how you feel about yourself. Does it leave you feeling constantly insecure and fearing that others will reject or abandon you? Or that they will do that if you ease up on trying to meet or exceed their standards?

Reflect more deeply on your socially prescribed perfectionism. Use your self-awareness in the domains of STEAM to help you understand your perfectionism more clearly. As described in the "Self-Evaluative Perfectionism" section above, for any domain in which you have difficulty, use the exercises in the chapter for that domain to help you. Journal about this, as well as your answers to these questions:

- *How much do you consider your own wants and needs when they don't align with what others might want?*

- *If expressing yourself is difficult, specifically what do you fear will happen by voicing your thoughts, feelings, desires, and beliefs?*

- *When you have expressed yourself with people who are supportive, what has happened?*

- *When you haven't expressed yourself, how has it affected your relationship and your sense of yourself—in good and bad ways? (This might be different in different relationships.)*

In developing a fuller appreciation of your socially prescribed perfectionism and its consequences, you will discover that you become more conscious of the negative effects on you.

If you engage in socially prescribed perfectionism, learning more about it will help you have greater appreciation of the struggle, enabling you to respond with empathy and compassion. As a result, your drive to be perfect for others will lessen and you will see yourself as worthy of love and acceptance. This might motivate you to consider your needs more seriously.

THE DOWNSIDE OF HIGH EXPECTATIONS

Mia had studied hard in high school, working to cover up her perception that she wasn't smart by demanding no less than an A for herself on all exams. So when she received one B and one C in her freshman year of college, she was horrified. *I'm so stupid. I don't belong here*, she repeated to herself. Believing these thoughts, she figured it was practically useless to study or ask for help. So, she didn't. Not surprisingly, her grades plummeted…which, of course, supported her original assumption that she was "stupid" and shouldn't bother wasting her time studying. In addition, her fear of being rejected by peers and fantasies of failing out of school increased.

Serena, who graduated in the top 10 percent of her high school class, also struggled with the transition to college. She feared she was incompetent, but she studied extra hard to overcome her perceived inadequacies. When, to her surprise, she did well in classes, she thought, *It's a good thing I studied so much. Now people won't think I'm dumb.* Though grateful for this, she was continually afraid that her secret would be discovered and everyone would look down on her.

Mia and Serena were unable to see the abilities they possessed, the ways that their fears of incompetence did not match the facts, and how unlikely it was that falling short of their high expectations would result in the dismal failure and rejection that they imagined. If you relate to either of these examples, think about how your self-perceptions and personal standards affect you.

Assess the Effects of Your High Expectations

Use these questions to help you explore how your personal standards and expectations affect you. You may want to write your answers in your journal. (If you have not reviewed the "Using Engaged Curiosity with Yourself" section of this chapter, do that now. By approaching these questions with engaged curiosity rather than with a critical eye, you will be more likely to gain greater insights by answering them.)

- How realistic do you think your standards for yourself are? How often do you meet them, and how does this affect you? Consider how this might differ in different areas of your life.

- Do you expect others to meet the same level of expectations you have for yourself? If not, what is your reasoning? Might this same reasoning apply to you?

- Consider a time when you fell short of your own standards. What did you think of yourself? What do you imagine others who care about you thought of you? What would you think about someone else if they made similar efforts and got the same results?

- When you do achieve success in meeting your standards, how do you feel about yourself? If you feel positively, how strongly and for how long? If you have a negative—or less than positive—reaction, what are your thoughts and feelings?

- If you go to extraordinary lengths to meet your goals and expectations— such as by working long hours or devoting all waking hours to them—how does this affect your sense of well-being, both emotionally and physically? Weigh the costs and benefits.

- How would your life be different if you gave significant effort toward your goals, but also allotted more time toward other personal interests and valued activities?

These questions can open up many avenues of self-exploration. So, you may want to work on them over several days, or even work on them a bit now and finish them at a later date.

MAKING PROGRESS AND CLARIFYING YOUR GOALS

For many reasons, your sensitivity to rejection can be overwhelming and disorienting. Because of this, you can easily lose your way in trying to escape from your struggles with rejection. Part of the problem is that this goal defines what you want to get away from, *not* what you want to move toward. So, to grow in ways that will feel constructive, fulfilling, and healthy, it is essential to define what you want to move toward.

Clarify Your Goals

Imagine your future self as enjoying a sense of well-being, free of rejection sensitivity. Then create a chart in your journal or on a loose piece of paper to clarify the goals and objectives that can help you create that reality and become more securely attached. You may also use the worksheet online at www.drbecker-phelps .com/home/bouncing-back/ or http://www.newharbinger.com/44024. Follow along with what Chad did to clarify his goals as an example for how you might do the same. (A chart showing Chad's work in this area is also online at www.drbecker -phelps.com/home/bouncing-back/ or http://www.newharbinger.com/44024.)

First, identify your goal: Chad wrote: Feel positively enough about myself that I don't assume Linda will leave me, can tolerate Linda being upset with me, and believe that I would survive my relationship with Linda ending (even if I'd be miserable for a while).

Then develop objectives for yourself based on STEAM.

- **Sensations:** Chad wrote: Feel physically less tense or more relaxed when talking with Linda and things objectively seem to be okay

- **Thoughts:** Chad wrote: Think more positively about myself in general; think positively about myself when I express a different opinion from Linda and other people

- **Emotions:** Chad wrote: Feel happier and at peace with myself in general; tolerate my fears of rejection enough to be able to get past them (rather than being totally sucked into them)

- **Actions:** Chad wrote: Tell Linda what I think when I disagree with her; do the same thing with other people

- **Mentalizing:** Chad wrote: Recognize what's going on for Linda rather than always assuming she's looking for a way to ditch me

Finally, ask yourself what is needed to happen for you to make progress. Chad realized that he needed to see how he was unnecessarily hard on himself and how he was too ready to believe others would reject him before he could begin to let go of his fears of rejection.

What Chad accomplished in clarifying his goals and objectives took time. It is easy to have a sense of what you want, but being specific in your plan requires focus and persistence. When what you desire most is to free yourself from being rejection sensitive, that effort is an important step toward lessening your reactivity to real or feared rejection, and increasing your resilience when you are hit hard by feelings of being dismissed or abandoned.

THE WISE CHOICE: BALANCING "SHOULDS" AND "WANTS"

Janine thinks about her friend Lucy, who can be a lot of fun. *But I'm done with lending her money that she never pays back,* Janine thinks. Now Lucy is asking to borrow money to pay a parking ticket—and Janine feels stuck. *Even though I should help her out because she's my friend, I don't want to. I feel like such a selfish person.*

Particularly because of your fear of rejection, you may find that you get easily frustrated or angry with yourself for not doing what you think you *should* be doing but don't really *want* to do. Then there is what you *want* to do but for some reason may not be a good idea to do. Finally, there is—if you take the time to think about it—what you believe is a *wise* choice, the best overall decision for yourself. This is the path that would ultimately be best to take.

You can help yourself make a wise decision by following these steps:

1. Listen to the negative, critical "should" voice as though it were external, coming from another person. Make note of the reasons this voice gives for insisting that you take action. Importantly, note how that voice discounts or minimizes *your* feelings and desires.

> Janine reflected: *I'm conscious of part of me saying, "You should give Lucy the money. I can't believe you are so selfish that you would say no and then go out to dinner with other friends."* Considering that critical voice within herself, she thought, *This line of thinking considers Lucy, but doesn't care about me or what's right for me.*

2. Attend to what you feel or want. Allow yourself to be open to the emotions and desires you experience deep within. Rather than focusing on your response to the critical voice, such as feeling guilty, attend to emotions that are direct from your inner true self.

> Janine was aware that she did not want to give Linda money. *I feel taken advantage of, and I don't want to be Lucy's personal bank.*
>
> This awareness did not come easily, though. At first, Janine was confused about her feelings. She originally thought, *I should not have to be someone's personal bank.* By using the word "should," she was focusing more on the way she expected the world to work, instead of embracing how she felt and what she wanted. But then she refocused on her feelings and replaced the word "should" with the word "want," which made all the difference. She clearly felt better about herself when she acknowledged, *I*

want to feel more assertive and empowered. And I don't want to be Lucy's personal bank.

3. *Take the time to make a wise decision.* Weigh your differing thoughts and feelings, the various potential actions you could take, and the potential outcomes for each act. This process can help you make the best decision given all that you know at the current time.

> Janine reasoned: *It is important to be there for friends, but my sense that I "should" give Lucy the money is misplaced. She has been using me, not being a good friend to me. So, I really think it's okay that I'd rather spend it enjoying myself with other friends. If she chooses not to talk with me, I can survive that, even though I'll feel awful. It's time that I finally say no and take the risk of losing her friendship.*

4. *Take action.* Once you know your chosen direction, it is important to take action, even if that means just developing a plan to help you move forward.

> Janine sensed that she needed to help herself follow through. *I think I'll talk with Beth before I say no to Lucy. I know she'll support me. It might even help if we make plans to get together later, after I've talked with Lucy.*

In any given situation, making a wise choice is a decision that you may need to make again and again. Encourage yourself to consider both your thoughts and your feelings in deciding what is ultimately best for you.

This type of dilemma comes up often in romantic relationships, too. For instance, Belinda—a twenty-six-year-old advertising copywriter, who felt deeply in love—had to talk herself through a breakup with her abusive boyfriend.

> Belinda thought: *My friends all tell me I should leave Paul because of the way he treats me, but I love him and feel like I'll forever have a*

broken heart if I leave. I'm such a weak person and a fool for staying with him!

Still, when I pay attention to how I feel, I see that he is mean to me and hurts me a lot. I'm forever afraid of making him angry. I have even begun to believe that I deserve how he treats me. I want to stay because I love him, but I also know I should leave. And I logically know that my friends would support my decision to leave. I'm so afraid of walking away, but I would eventually be happier without him. So I really have to go.

Belinda also talked with friends to rally support for leaving Paul. She planned out when and how she would tell him, as well as how she would fill her time after leaving.

EXPLORING CONSEQUENCES

Mentalizing involves reflecting on how the first four domains of awareness (sensations, thoughts, emotions, and actions) affect each other and are related to your rejection sensitivity. It will enable you to gain greater insight into yourself.

The following exercise, broken into three parts, is designed to help you with this very process. Because there is a lot to it, read through it all and look at Janine's sample chart (in the example after the directions for this exercise) before getting started.

Understand Yourself Through STEAM

In this exercise, you will be reflecting on your thoughts in a chart as you attend to your sensations, emotions, and actions. (A template for this exercise is also available online at www.drbecker-phelps.com/home/bouncing -back/ or http://www.newharbinger.com/44024.)

1. *Write the word "Sensations" at the top of a page in your journal (or on a piece of paper).*

   On the next line, write, "When I struggle with rejection or the fear of it, I often sense in my body..."

Below this, draw a line down the middle of the paper and write "Positive Sensations" on one side and "Negative Sensations" on the other side.

Now complete the chart with as many responses as come to mind. To help you connect with your sensations, you might find it helpful to bring to mind the struggles you identified in the exercise "Connect with Common Struggles" in chapter 4.

Finally, think about how the sensory consequences of your struggles with rejection affect your life. Jot down some notes about this at the bottom of the page.

2.   *Repeat the same steps for your emotions.* Instead of "Sensations," write the word "Emotions" at the top of a page. Replace "I often sense in my body" with "I often feel."

3.   *Label a third page with the word "Actions."* Replace "I often sense in my body" with "I often act by." Again, repeat the same steps as before.

4.   *For all three pages, reflect on and explore any outcomes that you note along the bottom of the pages.* Ask yourself whether and how they ultimately reinforce your struggles with rejection. For instance, on the emotions page, you might note that feeling angry with yourself is associated with being self-critical, which motivates you to be an especially good friend or to try hard to be the person you think your partner wants you to be.

While you can complete the whole exercise in one long session, you might prefer to spend a few days to complete each of the three sections. However you choose to complete the exercise, you may find that you continue to process it for days, if not longer.

To give you an idea of what your chart might look like, take a look at what Janine wrote when she was working on increasing her self-awareness through mentalizing. (A chart showing Janine's work in this area is also online at www.drbecker-phelps.com/home/bouncing-back/ or http://www.newharbinger.com/44024.)

Understand Yourself Through STEAM: Janine's Example

Sensations	
When I struggle with rejection or the fear of it, I often sense in my body…	
List "positive" sensations +	List "negative" sensations -
Energized (to prove myself) Alert	Headache Tension in my chest
My thinking about rejection often makes me feel tense and physically not well. That makes it hard to concentrate at work or enjoy myself with friends. Though it can make me feel alert, that's a heightened sense of looking to protect myself—I think this is my way of trying to protect myself from getting hurt.	

While insights from mentalizing are earned through hard work, newly attained ones can sometimes also be easy to lose. So, to help you remember and reinforce your insights, you might want to journal about them or talk about them with a friend or therapist. When others are supportive of such inner exploration, you will find the experience validating.

CHAPTER 8

Building Self-Acceptance

Janine is all too aware of her belief that she doesn't have much to offer others. *At least I'm a good friend,* she often repeats to herself as she tries to fend off the feeling that current friends will soon leave her behind. But recently, as she has been paying increasing attention to the different levels of self-awareness in STEAM, she has been having doubts about her belief that she's essentially worthless. She has also begun having the fleeting thought, *Maybe feeling worthless is just a feeling.* From there, the doubt has grown stronger as she has found herself repeating the statement, *Just because I feel worthless, it doesn't mean I am worthless.* At first this was almost unbearably uncomfortable. It felt wrong. Yet, she could not deny that she was a caring person and a good friend, and that she had friends who really cared about her. She also could not deny that she had good skills as a painter, though she would visibly wince when she remembered one teacher calling her "gifted." With her efforts to connect to, and accept, these positive experiences of herself, she began to feel the stirrings of self-acceptance.

For many of us, our rejection of ourselves is central to our struggles with rejection from others. You may find yourself doing this by blocking out or disconnecting from your basic experiences, a problem that can be overcome by reconnecting with the guidance of the STEAM chapters in this book. More broadly speaking, you may reject your general sense of your "true" self. This chapter offers ways for you to connect with, and be more accepting of, the person you experience yourself to be.

To be successful with this, it's essential that you accept two basic premises. First, human beings are, by nature, imperfect. We all have weaknesses and flaws and make mistakes. We all experience an array of emotions, including different kinds of emotional pain, such as hurt or grief. Researcher Kristin Neff (2011) describes this as a *common humanity*, and she explains that it is a necessary part of experiencing self-compassion (which will be explored in the next chapter).

The second premise may seem absurd to even have to state outright, but—you are a human being, with all the qualities that this implies. Most notably, being human means that you have weaknesses and flaws, make mistakes, and experience emotional pain. As basic as this may seem, this premise is likely to be more difficult for you to embrace. To fully accept it means that you struggle, suffer, and are sometimes rejected, not because there is something inherently wrong with you, but because these experiences are inherent in being human.

The exercises in this chapter encourage you to accept your full humanity, including all of your qualities. They will help you connect with and appreciate aspects of yourself that feel good. They also encourage you to accept your struggles as part of being human. The more you can build self-acceptance, the more positively you will feel about yourself, even with your weaknesses, flaws, and the mistakes you make. Importantly, you will also be less preoccupied with others rejecting you.

USING SELF-AFFIRMATIONS TO STAY POSITIVE

You can ease your struggles with rejection by using *self-affirmations*. Developed by psychologist Claude Steele (1988), this concept suggests that thinking about important values can help you maintain a positive sense of yourself when you feel threatened. The "values" he refers to can be anything about yourself that makes you feel good or proud, such as a trait, an ability, or a basic belief about what is important in life. *It's not that self-affirmations increase your self-esteem, but rather that they help you keep a positive feeling you already have about yourself by bringing your focus there.*

Janine acknowledges that she is a capable painter and a caring person—though she is uncomfortable doing so. When she directs her attention to these positive traits, she notices that she feels more positively about herself. Though she continues to fear that she will be rejected by friends and eschewed by coworkers, the intensity of these fears lessens. She is also more likely to feel warmed by positive feedback, like when her gym buddy Gina one morning let out an impressed, "You are so toned. You look great!"

Research has shown that by engaging in self-affirmations, people are less defensive and more accepting of emotionally challenging feedback (McQueen and Klein, 2006). While self-affirmations are unlikely to cure you of your sensitivity to rejection, they can lessen it. You might find that by feeling positively about yourself, you are less likely to so quickly assume others will see you in a negative light. And when someone does clearly take issue with something you have done or is critical of you, self-affirmations might help you to hold on to positives about yourself, enabling you to be resilient.

List Your Strengths

To develop and use self-affirmations, first identify your traits, talents, and values by creating three lists. Following the prompts below, write these in your journal (or on other paper).

As you brainstorm about these three aspects of yourself, you might be inclined to leave "unimportant" things off the list—DON'T. Include everything. Perhaps you are a good friend, a talented cook, or have great hair. You may minimize these qualities, but they are there. (Before you write off something like having great hair as being "too superficial" to feel good about, think about how critical you are for other "superficial" shortcomings, like a shrill karaoke voice.) *All* of your positives are affirmations of you as a whole person.

List traits about yourself that you value. For instance, you might think that you are funny, persistent, curious, caring, social, creative, or logical.

List your talents. For instance, you might include being a good carpenter, negotiator, or comforter to those in distress.

List the basic values that you live by. Examples of these are honesty, integrity, compassion, or generosity.

By completing your lists, you created a pool of inner resources that you can use for self-affirmations.

Affirming Your Positives

With your three lists, you can now start practicing self-affirmations. Try any or all of the ways below.

Reflect on your positives. Choose just a few (no more than six) of the positive aspects of yourself that are *most important to you*. They can include aspects from all or even just one of the categories.

Set aside some quiet time—even just 5 minutes—to think about these traits, talents, or values. Reflect on specific experiences that highlight them. If you become distracted by other thoughts, memories, or fears of failure or rejection, choose to redirect your thoughts to these self-affirmations. The purpose of this self-affirmation practice is to connect with aspects of yourself that you are proud of or that make you feel good about yourself.

Create a mantra. Many people find it helpful to develop a mantra that they repeat daily, based on something they value about themselves. For instance, Janine found it helpful to repeat, "I am a caring, empathic person." Your mantra might be: "I am an insightful, thoughtful person," or "I am creative."

Write about the aspect of yourself that you value most. It should be particularly meaningful to you and make you feel proud or good about yourself. Be sure to answer these questions fully:

- What is this value or aspect of yourself?

- Why is this value important?

- Describe times when you lived this value, including how it made you feel or what made it meaningful.

After completing this description for one value, you might want to do this self-affirmation practice again, focusing on another value.

Throw Out the Negatives

Looking specifically at people's body images, researchers Briñol and his colleagues (2013) conducted a study in which they focused on whether they could influence these perceptions. They directed subjects to write down what they liked about their bodies on one list and what they did not like about their bodies on a separate list. Then they were directed to throw out one of the lists. When they threw out a list (either one), they were less influenced by it. However, when they put a list in their pocket, they were more influenced by that one.

Although this study specifically focused on physical attributes, you may find a similar result with listing other qualities. Strengthening your positive sense of yourself may help you overcome your struggles with rejection.

A Pocketful of Positives

Refer to what you wrote down in the exercise "List Your Strengths." Then grab two loose pieces of paper. You can also complete this exercise using your smartphone, though many people find that the act of physically writing their thoughts can be therapeutic in itself.

Write a list of positive qualities about yourself on one of the pieces of paper. You can include anything, such as physical characteristics, personality traits, or skills you have acquired.

Write a list of qualities about yourself that you do not like on the other piece of paper. Write this quickly, being careful not to spend too much time elaborating on your negatives.

Throw out (or delete) the second list (of negatives).

Place the first list (of positives) in your pocket. Or save it on your phone. Either way, carry it with you for at least one full day, though you might want to carry it with you even longer than that.

To make this exercise more effective, consciously engage with it each day. At the end of the first day that you complete it, take the paper out of your pocket and review the list. The next morning, read it slowly before placing it back in your pocket for that day. Continue doing this daily until you feel that it is ingrained in your sense of self.

Give Yourself Permission to Feel Good and Get Going

Although Chad continued to enjoy playing baseball recreationally long after his high school championship days, he no longer does. His head has become too filled with thoughts like, *What if I lose my mechanics and just can't execute my curveball? If I let the guys down, they'll never forgive me.*

If, like Chad, you have trouble accepting positive aspects of yourself because you are so dominated by negative self-perceptions, you can increase your self-acceptance by engaging in activities that you enjoy. While they might be passions that you pour yourself into, this is far from necessary. The small pleasures or comforts in life are also important. But it's not enough to just perform these activities; you must also allow yourself to *feel* good. When you are enjoying the thought of doing an activity, actually engaging in it, or even reminiscing about it, you are much less likely to get caught up in negative perceptions of yourself or feelings of rejection.

There are four basic elements to enjoying activities. To help infuse your life with them, try the following:

1. *Identify your comforts, joys, and passions:* There are an infinite number of activities that might bring positive feelings. For example, you might want to play games on your phone, go for a car ride, take a stroll through a park, or plan a romantic date. (A longer, more complete list of enjoyable activities can be found at www.drbecker-phelps.com/home/bouncing -back/ or http://www.newharbinger.com/44024.) List those that you find pleasurable in your journal, on a separate sheet of paper, or on your phone. Then, write down any activities you enjoy that are not on the list.

List of Enjoyable Activities

Listen to music	Daydream	Plan a vacation
Watch a funny movie	Go out to dinner	Play miniature golf
Do a puzzle	Volunteer	Go for a drive
Help others	Get a massage	Drink coffee, or tea
Dance	Do landscaping	Browse a bookstore
Bicycle	Fix something	Cook
Learn a new skill	Do crafts	Play cards

2. Get moving: The next step is to get started on whichever ones you want to do, or feel most manageable to start with.

If you are in a negative or depressed state of mind, you might think that doing enjoyable activities is beyond what you are capable of. You don't have the energy or motivation. Fortunately, people are wired in a way that engaging in activities often gives them energy and can prompt positive feelings. So, choose an activity that is not too challenging and give it a try. Feel free to start by doing it a little at a time.

There are also some other ways you can help yourself get started. Planning an activity with a friend can help you feel more positively about it and discourage you from backing out. Another option is to give yourself permission to bail from the activity after you've given it a try.

> Chad had been feeling really down when March rolled around, so he was thinking he might just pass on signing up for baseball this year. He knew that being on the mound again in the spring would probably help him feel better, but he wasn't up to it. Finally, he decided to give it a try, promising himself that he would drop out if it didn't go well. Though he tended to be self-critical, he recognized there were times when he enjoyed just being out on the field with the team, smelling the freshly mown grass. Also, it wouldn't hurt to see that all the other guys were not as good as they had been in their younger days, either.

3. Enjoy the moment: As you do the things you like, you will hopefully feel naturally energized and engaged. However, many people struggle with the "what ifs," just as Chad did. *What if I've gotten too old to pitch? What if I let the guys down?* Once you recognize that you are doing this, choose to refocus on the moment. Attend to what you are doing *now*. Let the future take care of itself—even when that future is in just a few moments, as it was for Chad when he was worrying about facing the other team's best hitter in the next inning. If you realize you enjoyed the moment, even just a little bit, pause and allow yourself to absorb that positive.

Observe how your fears or feelings of rejection have a less powerful hold on you—and might have even disappeared for a time. Maybe you feel a little lighter, even if you do not exactly feel happy. Also, consider whether you were, for at least part of the time, engaged in what you were doing and not focused on your negative self-perceptions or fears of rejection.

4. Think about pleasurable experiences: As you look at the activities you listed, remember occasions when you enjoyed them. Really take the time to allow your memories to be detailed and to *feel* the experience again. Also, think about how you would like to do it again. Similarly, as you consider trying another activity, allow yourself to anticipate the experience.

By using some or all of these strategies, you are helping yourself initiate and have good experiences. Your interests, choices to act on those interests, and the enjoyment you get from them are all part of you. The more you can "own" them as part of you, the more you will feel good about yourself, and the more you will feel good about sharing those parts of yourself with others.

VIEW YOURSELF AS YOU WOULD A FRIEND

When Maya's five-year-old daughter asked for the tenth time where they were going, Maya snapped, "How many times do I need to tell you?!" And on she went about how her daughter never listens. After a few minutes, she came to her senses. *Damn!*

I did it again. I feel like such an awful mother, Maya lamented. But then, remembering the inner work she had been doing, she imagined her friend Elise under similar pressures she had been having, including not sleeping well. Maya realized that rather than being critical of Elise, she could really "get" how her friend would have lost it in that moment.

While Maya could relate to another mother's humanity by understanding her struggle, she viewed herself as essentially flawed—and a cause for criticism. By learning to see herself as a human being—no more, no less—she made strides in becoming more accepting of herself. As a result, she then had greater self-empathy and self-compassion.

The following exercise can help you to approach yourself as you would a friend.

Be Your Own Best Friend

You can learn to approach yourself with greater self-acceptance by doing the following:

Think of a friend who is in a situation that is similar to one you struggle with, and for which you are self-critical. If you can't think of a similar situation, then simply use your imagination.

Pay attention to your reaction. Notice how you are more understanding of how your friend's reaction is "only human," and so you have empathy and compassion for their struggle. If you are judgmental rather than empathic, spend more time trying to understand how your friend's experiences led to their reaction.

Try seeing yourself through that same lens. Pay attention to any shift toward feeling more empathy or compassion for yourself—even if the feelings only last a moment.

Approaching yourself with greater self-acceptance takes practice. You will find that you can do it better sometimes than other times. But with perseverance, you can build your ability to tolerate your feelings, understand your own behaviors and struggles, and respond more constructively to feelings of rejection.

If your efforts fail to elicit empathy for yourself, you may need to return to trying this approach after working more on developing your basic self-awareness in the different domains of STEAM.

LOOK AT YOURSELF FROM THE OUTSIDE IN

When you become easily overwhelmed by a particular memory of rejection, viewing yourself from the outside (as you did in the last section) can help you develop greater resilience. It can help decrease the intensity of your emotions, as well as increase your tolerance of them.

The difficulties caused by your emotions being out of a tolerable range cannot be underestimated. If you have not read (or do not remember) the "Staying in Your Window of Tolerance" section of chapter 2, do that now. It explains the different ways your body reacts to being overcome with feelings of rejection.

The following exercise offers you a way to view particularly painful memories of rejection from the outside, thus helping you better tolerate your emotions and expand your window of tolerance. Given that this is a more advanced exercise, make sure that you first do some work on increasing your awareness in the domains of sensations, thoughts, emotions, and actions. Also, given that the exercise can be emotionally triggering, you may find it helpful to at least briefly review chapter 2 sections "Learning to Self-Soothe" and "The Many Ways You Can Benefit from Mindfulness" because they offer ways to remain in (or return to) your window of tolerance.

Play a Movie in Your Mind

You will be going to the movies in your mind—or having a "movie-like" experience of a memory in which you struggled with feeling rejected. Just as you do in a real movie theater, you can watch the movie and get caught up in it—but with the comforting awareness that you are not truly in the action.

Decide on the event that you will want to watch. It can be a situation that has occurred or one that you fear will happen, such as your boss giving you a poor performance review. It's important to challenge yourself but not push yourself out of your window of tolerance. This exercise offers ways for you to make the experience more tolerable.

When you are ready to start, sit in a quiet spot where you will not be disturbed. Get comfortable and settle in. Close your eyes. Take a few deep breaths, inhaling through your nose and letting the air escape from your mouth, making the exhale longer than your inhale.

Imagine you are in a theater. You will be in charge of playing the movie, which will enable you to help yourself stay within your window of tolerance. You can make the experience less intense by pausing the movie, muting the sound, or even watching it in black and white. But fundamental to all of this is that you remember that you are just watching a movie in your mind's eye. Your goal is to be engaged enough that your arousal increases, but not so much that you end up outside your window of tolerance.

Practice this repeatedly, replaying the same situation until you can watch it through with increased—or even full—intensity and remain inside your window of tolerance.

To help you develop greater resilience to rejection in general, you can continue doing this with other incidents of rejection. If your memories are intrusive in your life and too intense to modify—or trying to do this exercise makes you very distressed—stop the projector. Depending on how intrusive and distressing these memories are in your life, you may want to find a therapist who can help you cope better with them.

LEARNING THE TRUTH: YOU ARE WORTHY AND ADEQUATE

You may struggle a lot with feeling like something is essentially wrong with you. Maybe you focus on shortcomings in your appearance or your intellect or some hard-to-identify problem. Whatever the issue is, the sense that your flaw keeps you from being equal to others feels so strong that you *know* it's true. And this is what makes you so sure that you will be rejected.

But what if you are wrong? What if you are basically no different from other people? This is not to say that you are without flaws or weaknesses. But what if everyone else has flaws? Maybe, just maybe, there is value in simply being the person you are. Not convinced? Imagine this:

> You are sitting under a tree at a local park. You see several elementary school-age children having fun together on a playground. Watching them run around, play on the swings, and slip happily down the slide brings a smile to your face. Then you notice a boy sitting on a bench off to the side. You become aware that he is watching the other kids intently, long-ingly, and uncomfortably. You imagine that he wants to join the fun but is afraid of being laughed at or ignored. In that moment, how do you feel toward him?
>
> Do you make judgments about how he lacks any value and is worthless? Do you think about what a loser he is? Or do you feel sorrow for his inner struggles, hoping that he can overcome his fears and join the others?

If your reaction is the latter one, wishing that he would join the others, then you inherently value him—even though he is not fulfilling his "responsibility" of playing and being social. You see him as worthwhile despite not having any knowledge of him *earning* that worth. All people have this same *inherent* worth—even you.

In thinking about this, you may find that you understand, even agree, but feel unable to apply it to yourself. That's okay. If this analogy does nothing more than open you to the possibility that you have worth, then that is a lot. Return to the image of that little boy from time to time, considering its implications for your worth.

Similarly, notice when you instinctively show caring toward others for their pain or struggles. You might observe this reaction in people you directly interact with, such as a colleague who is upset about a critical comment from a supervisor. Or you may challenge yourself to think about people you have a more distant relationship with, such as refugees in the news or sick people in a hospital you happen to be driving past. Consider how your sense of caring is based on your connection with them as fellow human beings, not based on specific contributions they've made to the world.

KINTSUGI: FIND BEAUTY IN YOUR BROKENNESS

The idea that you have value just for existing can be a difficult one to grasp, especially when you feel broken inside. Similarly, it can be difficult to fully grasp that your worth is not based on what you accomplish, especially when you perceive that you have not accomplished enough. To illustrate these elusive ideas, consider the art form of *kintsugi.*

Kintsugi is the Japanese art of rejoining the broken fragments of a piece of pottery with gold or other precious metals. While the repaired item may be aesthetically appealing, the real beauty is in how people relate to it. The beauty is in valuing the life of the ceramic, which includes the damage that happens over time.

Similarly, to truly value yourself, it is essential to value your life's journey. Mothers do this when they smile while looking at a stretch mark that they earned during the pregnancy of their child. Those who have endured childhood abuse do it when they appreciate that their sensitivity to others' pain comes from the pain they have endured. Each year, many Americans value their country's hard-won freedom when they honor veterans by visiting Arlington National Cemetery in Washington, D.C., or other landmarks that celebrate painful times in their history. It's important to note that appreciating brokenness or imperfection as part of your life story does not mean you "should" be happy about the pain that you have endured. But you can appreciate your strength in overcoming your struggles, find value in the lessons you have learned from them, and be grateful for the resilience you have built.

See Your Beauty

You can practice transforming your sense of brokenness into a beautiful new you by learning to relate differently to your struggles. To do this, follow these three steps:

Challenge what you find acceptable. Reconsider your belief that you need to be some particular way to have value. Reconsider the "given" that, to be worthy of acceptance or love by others, you must earn a certain amount of money, be charming or outgoing, have a particular body shape, excel at sports, or be a recognized talent.

Practice consciously accepting your limitations, weaknesses, or failures. Once you can accept that it's your belief in needing to be a particular way that's "flawed," then there is the possibility that your perceived imperfection may not be a valid reason for others to reject you.

Accept and appreciate yourself for who you are. Consider what it would mean to accept your perceived imperfection. Might you still have value as a person? Might others accept you anyway, or even value you in part *because* of your "imperfection"?

By practicing self-acceptance for all aspects of yourself, you create an opportunity to heal.

As you enjoy a more positive self-image, you will make steps toward overcoming your self-rejection and your sensitivity to rejection by others. Let's consider how Andrew, a systems analyst, learned to find beauty in his brokenness.

Challenge what you find acceptable. Andrew began to question how he derived so much of his worth from seeing himself as intelligent, logical, and able to solve any problem he faced. He could see how whenever he failed to fix a problematic relationship or practical issue, his self-esteem would spiral downward and he would often end up depressed. He would isolate himself from others because he feared that they would see he was unworthy of their friendship.

Practice consciously accepting your limitations, weaknesses, or failures. As Andrew focused on his need to fix every situation or problem, he realized that this required the impossible from him—to be all-knowing or all-powerful. With this realization, he became more aware of feelings of sadness and powerlessness about the things he could not change. He also began to question his reflexively negative thoughts about himself in response to when he felt powerless.

Accept and appreciate yourself for who you are. Andrew could appreciate his clear thinking, problem-solving abilities, and compassion for others. He also liked being able to make friends laugh. He realized that he did not have to "have it all figured out" to feel good about himself or for others to like him.

BE STRONG: ASK FOR HELP

For Janine, being inferior was a statement of fact, like saying that overcast days are gray. She tended not to talk with anyone about it, but when she lost a big client at work, it all came pouring out to her friend Beth. She related, "I just feel like I'm no good. I obviously wasn't any good at work. And I know this sounds pathetic, but I feel like I'm lucky that anyone even wants to hang out with me because I'm such a loser. I just feel so alone." She partly expected that Beth would never talk with her again, but then something surprising happened. "You are *not* a loser, but I do know how you feel. I'm always thinking about how my life is going nowhere. I feel scared and alone a lot," Beth shared. When they finished talking, both women felt less alone and a little less hopeless.

Many people fear that appearing weak and asking for help will drive others away. But everyone needs help sometimes. It's part of being human in the same way that having weaknesses and making mistakes are part of being human. Just as admitting to your struggles takes strength, it also takes strength to acknowledge when you are trying to lift a weight that is too heavy to carry alone.

Once you decide that you need help, be wise in choosing whom you will ask. You want to reach out to someone who is supportive, caring, and trustworthy. People who can remain calm while discussing emotional issues are likely to be better at helping you calm down. Also, look for signs that they want to be helping, such as calling you to check on how you are doing. Consider these tips for *how* to ask for help:

Choose an appropriate time. For instance, you may not want to ask your friend when they are preoccupied with their own immediate concerns. If you believe that it's a good time to talk, you might still ask before launching in.

Ask for what you need. People can help best when they know what's needed from them. So, be as clear as you can about whether you are looking for emotional support, advice, practical help, or something else.

Do your part in the conversation. If you are too overcome with emotion to think clearly, then just pour it out. But also be open to the support offered by your friend. If you are looking for advice, then truly listen to their proposed ideas and possibly brainstorm with them. The more open you are to the help you are requesting, the more likely your friend will want to keep helping, and the better the experience will be for both of you.

Finally, remember to be there for your friends. Though their problems may be different from yours, they will undoubtedly have struggles. Listen and be a support. In addition to feeling good, this can help you fully realize that you are not alone in sometimes needing help. When you nurture relationships in which you can look to each other in times of distress, those secure relationships can help you develop a general view (or model) of others as emotionally available. This change is a step toward being more securely attached and less driven by feelings and fears of rejection.

When struggles with self-worth and self-criticism overtake your mind and heart, you can do yourself a great service by consciously engaging inner resources or turning to outside help. Use the awareness you gain through STEAM to empathize and accept yourself. Also, choose to take in positive feedback from others. While increasing your self-acceptance will probably lead to greater self-compassion, at the least, it will open you to developing that resource, as discussed in the next chapter.

CHAPTER 9

Nurturing Compassionate Self-Awareness

"I love you," Chad said softly as he hung up the phone from Linda. While she was helping her mother recover from a stroke, he consciously kept his fears of rejection at bay by reminding himself, *She loves me.* He strained to stay present with his hard-won self-awareness: *My heart is beating fast because I'm scared of losing Linda…I wonder if she's interested in that old friend, Rob, who she keeps talking about…Stop it. I know that my fears of rejection from the past are leading me to think that she wants to leave me. But I also know from our conversations that this isn't true.* Then he reassured himself again, *She shows me all the time that she loves me.* With all of this awareness and self-talk, he calmed himself. But then the fears hit again. And the cycle just kept repeating itself. *Damn it! What is my problem?! I am such an ass for making a crisis out of a whole lot of nothing. If I keep this up, I deserve to lose her!*

While Chad has made progress in having a greater understanding of his struggles, he eventually makes his distress worse by chastising himself. It's interesting that he could maintain a more compassionate response to Linda. His heart ached for her sadness about her mother, and he wished he could do something—anything—to help ease her distress. If he had a similar feeling of compassion for himself, he would have recognized his own distress at not having been able to shed his fears of rejection despite sincere efforts. He would have gently assured himself, *Of course I'm afraid of losing Linda. She has been gone for a while and will now be gone longer. Though I've come a long way in not overreacting to my fears, it makes sense that this would push my buttons. If someone else were in my position, I'd understand them having a hard time with it. I deserve the same consideration. I just need to keep taking the time to think this through and to remind myself that we have a strong relationship.*

You nurture compassionate self-awareness when you learn to understand and approach yourself from a compassionate perspective—with empathy for your experience and a mind-set of wanting to alleviate your pain. This skill will enable you to help yourself remain on the path toward overcoming your struggle with rejection—even at times when you are inclined to be self-critical or get lost in your emotional pain.

To gain compassionate self-awareness, you must first develop increased self-awareness in the domains of STEAM. Hopefully this will help you have greater empathy for yourself and so gain self-acceptance, another essential element of self-compassion. However, even if you struggle with this, you can work to bolster your self-acceptance, as described in chapter 8. Finally, you must treat yourself with kindness and caring. That is, you must respond to your pain from an emotional place of caring that you are in pain and wanting it to stop.

You might wonder what the difference is between self-compassion and compassionate self-awareness. This is a good question because they are very similar concepts, though they differ in emphasis. Self-compassion emphasizes *treating yourself with kindness* when you are faced with pain and suffering. It also requires that you be aware of your experiences and can relate to them empathically. Compassionate self-awareness is more centered on awareness, with the word "compassionate" describing the quality of that awareness. It emphasizes *being empathically self-aware* when you are faced with pain and suffering. This can then motivate you to treat yourself with kindness and compassion.

People can often effectively practice self-compassion by choosing to be kind to themselves when they are distressed. However, many people are not fully in touch with their negative self-perceptions, which undermines their attempts to engage in self-compassion. They cannot empathize with their own experience (causing them to lack self-acceptance), and so they are not sufficiently motivated to treat themselves with caring or kindness. In these situations, it is essential that they focus on being more self-aware to help them transition to self-compassion. For instance, consider the personal growth that Chad made over the course of his relationship with Linda.

If Linda had to take care of her mother during the early days of their relationship, Chad would have been quickly overcome with feelings of rejection. Unable to gain perspective on his feelings, no amount of prompting to have self-compassion would have helped him respond differently. However, later in their relationship, after he learned to have greater self-awareness, he understood his reaction better, could see it in a way that loosened its grip on him, and had more empathy for that reaction. This opened him to having more self-compassion, or at least to being able to get there with some prompting.

This chapter focuses on adding self-kindness to the self-awareness and self-acceptance that has been developed in the other chapters. The first section explores the benefits of self-compassion while the next one addresses common struggles that people have in responding to themselves with compassion. Then the rest of the chapter guides you in how to consciously be kinder and more compassionate to yourself.

EXPLORING COMPASSION

Understanding more about compassion lets you better appreciate how it can help you overcome your sensitivity to rejection. Though compassion has a long history of being viewed in Buddhist thinking as essential in attaining enlightenment, Western therapies have tended to only assume or imply its importance in growth and healing. However, recent attention and research in the West have explored and developed this concept more.

As you may know or have discovered in reading this book, your personal history can have a huge impact on how you connect with yourself and with other people. British clinical psychologist Paul Gilbert (2009) has further found in his research that people's early experiences and their attachment styles can lead to shame and self-criticism, along with a weakness in their ability to comfort and soothe themselves. Fortunately, they can develop a sense of safety and inner warmth by learning the skills and attributes of compassion. Although Gilbert's work focuses broadly on compassion, it also delineates the importance of self-compassion in addressing self-criticism.

Interestingly, psychologist and self-compassion researcher Kristin Neff (2011) has found support for three main elements of self-compassion, which align well with Gilbert's attributes of compassion. These elements are similar to those found in compassionate self-awareness. They are mindfulness (similar to self-awareness), common humanity (relates to self-acceptance and mentalization), and self-kindness. So, although self-compassion is different than compassionate self-awareness, Neff's work has influenced, and overlaps with, the concept of compassionate self-awareness.

In looking at self-compassion and attachment styles, it is clear that they affect each other. By increasing your self-compassion, you can help yourself become more securely attached and less overly sensitive to rejection. Increasing self-compassion and secure attachment can also help you in many other ways (Neff and McGehee 2010, Wei et al. 2011, Barnard and Curry 2011, Hazan and Shaver 1987, Mikulincer and Shaver 2007). For instance, it can help increase:

- Positive feelings
- Self-acceptance
- Life satisfaction
- Conscientiousness
- Social connectedness
- Satisfaction and health of romantic relationships
- Effective stress management skills
- Sense of well-being

Increasing your self-compassion builds these strengths by enabling you to soothe yourself when you are upset, take in comfort when other people offer it, and develop resilience to stressful events, such as being overlooked, dismissed, or rejected.

SELF-COMPASSION IS NOT FOR ME

When you hear the word "self-compassion," do you internally pull back or put up a wall? If so, you are in good company. Many people respond this way for several different reasons—but all based on misconceptions of self-compassion (Neff and Germer 2017, Barnard and Curry 2011). Read each of the reasons below and follow the prompts to reflect on them.

Showing myself compassion would mean I'm self-centered. Many people worry that by taking care of themselves, they would be viewing themselves as the center of the universe. But the truth is that to sustain caring for others, you must take care of yourself.

Think about the safety instructions flight attendants give passengers in case of an emergency in which oxygen masks drop down: "If you are traveling with a child or someone who requires assistance, secure your mask first, and then assist the other person." Of course, the reason they say this is that you can't help anyone else if you pass out from lack of oxygen. So, remind yourself that you want to take care of yourself along with (*not instead of*) caring for others.

Some people neglect basic self-care, such as eating healthy, exercising, or getting enough sleep. Some forgo all things they enjoy in order to take care of others. Such selflessness can leave them low on energy, limited in their ability to care for themselves or others. It can also lead them to feeling negatively toward themselves or resentful toward others.

> *Take time to reflect:* If you are concerned that treating yourself with compassion would make you self-centered, take a moment to consider how ignoring or trying to reject your own experience has affected you, including your ability to care for others. Next, think about how attending better to yourself might affect your ability to be there for others.

Self-compassion is the same as self-pity. These concepts are very different. Even though they are both focused on the self, the difference is that only self-compassion includes self-acceptance and what Kristin Neff (2011) describes as a sense of common humanity—that all people are, by nature, imperfect and have painful emotional experiences.

Self-pity says, "Rejected again. I feel worthless and like a pathetic human being. There is something wrong with me." Self-compassion says, "Rejected again. As much as this hurts, I know other people get rejected, too. It's just part of being human."

While self-pity makes you feel alone and lesser as a person, self-compassion accepts your experience as a human one, meaning you are not alone in how you feel, and how you feel doesn't mean anything negative about you as a person.

> *Take time to reflect:* If you continue to be wary of self-compassion for fear of it leading to self-pity, try recognizing the common humanity in your struggles. Make note that others also struggle with rejection.

If I have self-compassion, I will become lazy. My patients will often say that they think being self-compassionate would "let myself off the hook." They fear that if they give up their tougher, more self-critical stance, they will just be lazy failures and no one would want to be around them.

While self-criticism sometimes can push people to work hard, it also makes them feel badly about themselves. When it comes to accomplishing tasks, they don't enjoy successes and often simply give up trying. On the other hand, when they are gently supportive of themselves, they feel good about themselves even as they are upset about a situation. Then they have more inner strength to keep trying to fix relationship problems or attend to tasks that are important to them.

> *Take time to reflect:* This way of thinking may be firmly entrenched, taking some time and persistence to shift. Continue to work on developing your ability to mentalize and increase your self-acceptance. You may find it particularly helpful to review the section "When Perfectionism Falls Short" in chapter 7, "Mentalizing."

I don't deserve compassion. Some people reject self-compassion because they feel worthless and inadequate. They are sometimes angry with others for treating them like they don't matter, but they also feel like they don't matter. In their minds, they don't deserve to be treated with kindness and understanding. Instead, as much as it hurts, they feel like they deserve rejection by others.

> *Take time to reflect:* If you relate to this struggle, return to the earlier chapters. It is important to work on increasing your self-awareness through STEAM and also on challenging yourself to be more self-accepting. You might find it particularly helpful to review the section "Learning the Truth: You Are Worthy and Adequate" in chapter 8, "Building Self-Awareness." Remind yourself to be patient, because it generally takes time and persistence to work through this issue. If you continue to strongly resist the idea that you have value even after working through many of the exercises in this book, consider seeking professional help, perhaps using this book as a template for approaching your therapy.

As you continue on your inner journey, you may repeatedly and instinctively balk at the ideas of getting to understand yourself better and approaching yourself with compassion. When you realize that you are being resistant, choose to think more about that resistance. By questioning your emotional reactions in the ways suggested here, you can keep yourself on the path toward developing compassionate self-awareness and becoming more resilient in the face of rejection.

LIVING A HEALTHY LIFESTYLE

> Just like many people who fear rejection, Janine was so focused on others that she didn't take good care of herself. There were times when she tried to develop a healthier lifestyle, such as eating healthier or exercising regularly, but it always ended up a miserable failure. She was only able to make and sustain some changes when she began thinking about her obstacles to change.

As you think about ways to strengthen the physical and psychological aspects of yourself, consider these fundamental elements of a healthy lifestyle:

- Sufficient sleep

- Healthy eating

- Regular exercise

- Strong social connections

- Connection to something larger than you (e.g., religion, spirituality, giving back to a community larger than yourself)

- Personally meaningful activities

Attending to these means attending to yourself, something that can be painfully difficult for people who are single-mindedly focused on preventing rejection or proving their worth. If you have trouble maintaining a healthy lifestyle, set aside some undisturbed time to complete the following exercise.

Create a Healthy Lifestyle

Think about the following questions and write down your responses in your journal (or on a piece of paper).

Why do I want to change? Reviewing this question can increase your motivation by focusing on what you want. So, give it some serious thought.

What needs to happen for me to lead my life in this way? You must change how you conduct your life in order to make room for any new healthy habit. Consider what changes you need to make to your life.

What feelings—and related thoughts—arise when I think about making these changes? You will have many different feelings. Take special note of the ones that you sense tap something deeper—especially issues of rejection, abandonment, or being inadequate.

What do I think about my feelings? Acknowledge your feelings, allowing yourself to understand them, and then consider what you objectively think.

How can I overcome the stumbling blocks to creating a healthy lifestyle? Reaffirm the changes you want to make. Also, keep in mind that this question is not just about what you need to do practically, but also how to manage your feelings.

How important is changing to me, and what makes it that important? Answering these questions can be motivating.

What is my plan going forward? Write down a specific plan, including details about each step and also addressing emotional issues.

Reviewing this plan regularly, such as once a week, can help you stay on track with it. You might also find it motivating to come up with a way to reward yourself for sticking with it.

Keep in mind that most people struggle in some way with leading a healthy lifestyle. However, with some introspection and planning, your efforts to change are much more likely to be successful. By understanding and accepting your needs, you will be more likely to be kind to yourself in attending to those needs. And when you do attend to those needs, you will feel better about you, even as you face concerns about rejection.

Let's consider how Janine established a healthier lifestyle for herself by looking at her journal entries in response to each question.

Why do I want to change? Despite struggling with her weight for years, Janine had been unsuccessful in maintaining healthy eating or regular exercise. Referring to the need to exercise, she wrote, "To help me lose weight—be stronger—feel healthier—be happier with myself."

What needs to happen for me to lead my life in this way? "To fit in exercise, I need to go to the gym before work, which means getting up at 5 a.m. The only way to really do this is to go to sleep earlier, maybe 9:30 p.m. But I have to be there for Gina on our nightly talks. I don't know if I'm really up for doing this."

What feelings—and related thoughts—arise when I think about making these changes? "I feel anxious at the thought of telling Gina I can't talk because I have to sleep. How lame is that?! I can't be that selfish. Gina will feel like I've let her down and would probably not want to talk with me anymore…"

What do I think about my feelings? "I can feel myself almost panicking as I think about losing Gina as a friend. I need to get a grip. My fear doesn't even make sense. I know in my head that Gina would not abandon me for this."

How can I overcome the stumbling blocks to creating a healthy lifestyle? "Two big obstacles are going to sleep earlier and not talking with Gina. First, the truth is that I could get to sleep earlier if I set my mind to it—even if that means spending less time on Facebook." Janine continued, "As for Gina, I'm sure she would work with me. Maybe I can even talk her into going to the gym with me! I'd really like that. Still, I feel anxious about talking with her. But I can do this. I'll talk with her later."

How important is changing to me, and what makes it that important? "I really want to feel and be healthier. And it would feel great to walk up steps easily—no huffing and puffing—and to be a size 8 again! When I think about it, I definitely feel motivated to exercise."

What is my plan going forward? Because Janine was so worried, she talked with Gina before sitting down to write out her plan. She was surprised to find that Gina agreed to go to the gym with her. She then wrote out her plan for getting to bed early and going to the gym four days a week. She finished up her journal entry with, "I'm excited to make this happen. I'm also excited about our plan to have lunch together every Friday to celebrate another week of keeping our commitment!"

COMPASSIONATE SELF-AWARENESS IN A SINGLE PHRASE

Self-awareness enables you to understand and connect with your inner experiences. When it opens you sufficiently to those experiences, you will feel empathy with them. And as a result, when your experiences are painful, you will often feel self-compassion—which will challenge your self-rejection.

Compassionate self-awareness is the process of opening up to this caring connection within yourself. It is the realization of a beauty that is already inside you, much as a flower is the realization of the beauty held within a bud. You know that you are experiencing compassionate self-awareness when you find it natural to say, "Of course I ..."

> "Would it be okay if we met a little later, at 8 o'clock, because I think Donna and I will need a bit more time to catch up." Rather than asking a question, Linda seemed to be simply checking off items on her to-do list. But Chad's heart was suddenly pounding hard and he felt like inhaling required the same effort and concentration as lifting weights. Just as he was about to explode into a full panic, he had a flash of insight (based on all the self-awareness work he had been doing). He saw what was happening and reassured himself: *She is not trying to get rid of me. She just wants enough time for them to catch up; and then she wants to spend time with me...I can't believe how much I'm overreacting!... I'm always so worried about not being good enough. This goes all the way back to when I was a kid and I felt like I could never be as smart as my brothers—and like my parents were disappointed in me. And to make things worse, I was also so painfully shy with other kids—feeling on the outside all the time. Given all this, of course I am starting to panic—anyone in my position would. It's a painful way to be wired, but I will survive it. Also, Linda doesn't need me to be outgoing or a genius, or anything else. She shows me all the time that she loves me.*

As you consider an example of your own sensitivity to rejection, the next exercise will help you make sense of your reaction. For instance, you might realize that you were affected by dynamics in your family when you were growing up. Or you might think about how you have been affected by friendships, or by previous intimate relationships. You are not looking to say whether your reactions—past or present—are good or bad. You are just trying to understand and empathize with them enough for it to be natural for you to say, "Of course I..."

Practice Responding to Yourself with an Empathic "Of course I…"

Think of a specific incident when you struggled with rejection. As you do, consciously empathize and offer compassion to yourself by doing the following:

Attend to the first four domains of STEAM. Rather than just quickly touching on each domain, allow yourself time to really connect with each experience—enriching your self-awareness as a whole.

Mentalize to understand and empathize better with yourself. After the initial step of increasing your self-awareness, reflect deeply on your reaction so that you can experience compassion for your struggles with rejection. For example, consider how previous life experiences play a part in your current reaction. If you are caught up in self-criticism, you might think about how a supportive friend would respond to your feeling of rejection if they fully understood what you were feeling and what influenced you to feel this way.

Respond with "Of course I…" When you are able to empathize with your struggle with rejection, complete this phrase by explaining to yourself how your reaction is a human one. It is a reaction that others in your situation would also have. Allow for the natural compassionate feelings of wanting your struggle to diminish or go away.

When you feel compassionately toward yourself, you will be in a position to make better decisions about how to proceed. Rather than being critical of your sensitivity to rejection, you will be more understanding of it, which will free you to focus on how best to move forward.

When you gain compassionate self-awareness, you may also become more open to compassion from others. As a result, you may move toward a more secure attachment style, which would be less fraught with struggles related to rejection.

USING YOUR PRESENT SELF TO HELP YOUR FUTURE SELF

As with so much in life, there is a rhythm to our emotions. Every day, there are the small undulations of uplifted and downhearted moments. In a single interaction, you can even be carried from loneliness to connection, or from restless unease to exhilarating love. But, of course, it's the downside of emotions that are more often upsetting. When the weight of rejection pins you down, it can feel like there is no way—and will never be a way—to escape it. You can so lose touch with the positive moments that they feel unreal and unachievable. Fortunately, even in those desperately low moments, your positive experiences are still in you—you just need to reach them.

The next exercise offers you a way to help your future dejected self by guiding you through writing a letter to that self. When Linda was spending time away from Chad while caring for her mother, Chad was glad that he had previously taken the time to write this letter. He realized that he was able to turn inward for comfort in times of distress (essentially serving as his own attachment figure). You might be able to see from the letter pictured below how reading it over was able to help when he was struggling.

Hey, Buddy. The fact that you are reading this means you are in a dark place right now. You are probably feeling worthless—like dirt—and that no one really cares about you. And I'm really sorry about that—it's a tough place to be. But the truth is that when you get in this place, everything looks worse than it is. Even though you aren't feeling good now, there have been times when you have felt good—and there will be times when you will feel that way again. Think about what you know to be true about the people in your life—you have friends who have always been there for you. Linda has shown you, over and over again, that she cares. So, even though you feel worthless right now, remember that is just a feeling that will pass. Sometimes it has helped to call Linda, a friend (maybe Scott?), or to go to the batting cages. Do those things or focus on something else that helps you feel good. I promise you that you will feel better and stronger again.

Me.

Write a Letter to Your Future Self

This exercise offers a way for you, while in your best state of mind, to help yourself when you feel overwhelmed by rejection. To complete the exercise, choose a time when you are feeling positively about yourself. Then follow these steps:

Before writing to your future self, reflect on a time when you felt overwhelmed by rejection. As an outside observer, note how the rejection took over your emotions and your thinking. Not only did it prevent this past self from feeling anything positive, but it also distorted almost everything about you and your experiences to make it all seem to be awful.

Note your thoughts about, and feelings toward, that past self. It is important to do this as an outside observer, one who is currently feeling good about yourself. When you focus on your past self, think about how your struggles were human ones. Then you will notice that you are better able to have empathy and compassion for that past self.

Consider what advice you would want to offer that past self. Think in terms of what that self could do to try to get through this difficult time. For example, you might suggest calling a friend or going for a walk.

Now write the letter to your future distressed self. Put all of your answers to the above questions together in a letter offering your future upset self some compassion, encouragement, and even a bit of advice while going through a similarly difficult time.

Put the letter in an accessible place. When the day comes that you are again struggling deeply with rejection, open the letter. You will find that it helps. After all, who knows and understands you better than you!

Part of what makes this letter helpful is that you know deep in your heart that the person who wrote the letter understands you, honestly cares, and is being truthful in saying that the negative feelings won't last forever (despite how it feels).

DEVELOPING SELF-COMPASSION TAKES TIME

Compassionate self-awareness requires caring enough about yourself that you want to get to know you. While you may want to shed your fears of rejection and enjoy a happier life, you may not quite be at the point where you feel compassionately toward yourself. Or maybe you have moments of having self-compassion, but your frustrations and self-criticisms often override them. Still, you can imagine that there could be a time when you do have more self-compassion. This imagining can be a source of strength as you confront your struggles with rejection.

Imagine a Compassionate You

By drawing upon the skills you have learned throughout this book, this exercise focuses your imagination on what it would be like to have self-compassion, thus actually increasing that very ability.

Think of your increasing self-awareness. Reflect on how increasing your self-awareness in the domains of STEAM has helped you have more empathy with your struggles with rejection. Note the self-acceptance that has been emerging as you have felt empathic toward yourself. Also pay attention to any glimpses of self-compassion you have had along with your growing empathy and self-acceptance.

Think about all the elements of a compassionate person. It may help to recall people you have known or heard about who are compassionate. For example, you might bring to mind a parent, an aunt, a mentor, or a friend. You might also think about a religious figure (such as Jesus or Buddha), a political figure (such as Nelson Mandela), or even a character from a novel or a film. List the qualities that you notice, such as warmth, caring, acceptance, and understanding.

Imagine your future self as compassionately self-aware. Imagine what your older self might look like from the outside, including your countenance and what you would be wearing. See that future self as being understanding and at peace. This self knows everything you have ever thought, felt, and done. With a deep understanding of you, this self feels positively toward you.

Settle into a memory of rejection. Sit comfortably, close your eyes, and turn your attention inward. Attend to the position of your body and your breath. Think of the word "rejection" and allow memories of feeling rejected to come to you. Settle on one memory. Stay with it until you feel it strongly, in body and emotions.

Imagine your future compassionate self coming to you. This future you clearly feels warmth toward you and shares an understanding of you from a compassionate perspective. The message may be offered in words, a look, or some gesture. But however it is shared, you can feel the acceptance and compassion deeply. Take a moment to consciously absorb this experience.

Thank your compassionately aware future self. As the interaction draws to a close, thank your compassionate future self. As you say goodbye, take note of the positive feeling you have within you.

After doing this exercise, reflect on it. Note how the compassionately self-aware future self is evolving in you at this moment. As you continue to work on enhancing your compassionate self-awareness, you are actually nurturing that self now.

(If you find it too difficult to imagine yourself being compassionate, you may find it helpful to first try this exercise with one of the figures you thought of when you reflected on the elements of compassion. After successfully doing the exercise with that person, you might try again with your future self.)

BE ON THE LOOKOUT

Your struggles with rejection run deep because connection is at the core of our experiences as people. For this reason, stories that explore the depths of people's intimate lives—within themselves or with others—speak directly to our psyches. They can tap our deepest pains and our most treasured aspirations.

You can use this natural portal into the raw emotional experiences of others as a way to help you connect with, and relate to, your own struggles. So, be on the lookout for stories—such as in the form of books or movies—that you can relate to. You might find this experience in timeless romantic classics, such as Shakespeare's *Romeo and Juliet*, or movies about self-discovery, such as *Bridget Jones's Diary* or *Thelma & Louise*. You might also find it in personal stories reported in the news. Use the stories that move you as a way to deepen your connection with your inner experiences, enabling you to better understand your struggles and have compassion for them.

Developing compassionate self-awareness is a process. It involves an evolution from self-awareness to self-empathy and self-acceptance, and ultimately to self-compassion. Being compassionately self-aware is a skill that you develop and then must choose to use again and again to free yourself from your struggles with rejection and other challenges.

CHAPTER 10

Recovery Through Relationships

Janine looked mindlessly at the menu, waiting as patiently as she could for Beth, who was late, yet again. When Beth finally came in and settled into her chair, Janine quickly got over her friend's tardiness and poured out, in animated excitement, her plan for a new business. "You know the empty store on Pine Street? Well, I know I'm being ridiculous and will probably be in way over my head, but I want to turn it into a café art gallery. I want to hang the paintings of local artists—*including mine*—and have a wall with books. The store has a small courtyard in the back that I could arrange for outdoor seating and even have some local musicians play. So, what do you think?" As she expected, Beth was enthusiastically supportive, and they immediately began brainstorming about how to make it happen.

When there was a lull in the conversation, Janine sat back and mused about her efforts at personal growth in the last couple of years. Her mouth unconsciously curled into a knowing smile as she realized just how much more open, happy, and adventurous she had become, and how much her friends had been a part of that growth.

After giving so much attention in this book to self-awareness in the domains of STEAM, it is important to consider the part your relationships can play in overcoming your sensitivity to rejection. As was addressed in chapter 1, attachment theory emphasizes the importance of developing a positive relationship with yourself and with *attachment figures* in your life. As a reminder, attachment figures are significant people in your life whom you turn to during times of distress.

Throughout this book, you have been guided in reflecting upon your relationships with yourself and with other people. You may remember that attachment theory explains that people develop a *model of self* in which they tend to see themselves as somewhere on a range from worthy and lovable to unworthy and unlovable. They also develop a *model of others* (based on experiences with past and present attachment figures) in which they tend to see others somewhere on a range from emotionally available to emotionally unavailable. The combination of these two models you hold within you has significant implications for how you cope with your emotions and respond to difficulties, and for the quality of the relationships in your life.

People with a secure style of attachment enjoy close, healthy relationships without worrying too much about rejection. They feel worthy and see others as emotionally available. When they are rejected or at least perceive that they are, they can feel deeply distressed, but not generally to the point of feeling it is intolerable. They are also resilient, able to bounce back and move on with their lives.

You can enjoy the benefits of being more securely attached by learning to see significant people in your life as attachment figures who can consistently offer a sense of safety and support. Attachment theory suggests that when you do this, these attachment figures serve three essential functions, each of which is explained in detail later in this chapter:

1. *Proximity* refers to the physical and psychological closeness of an attachment figure.

2. *Safe haven* refers to the sense that an attachment figure provides protection and comfort when someone feels threatened or distressed.

3. *Secure base* refers to when an attachment figure offers support for exploring experiences (e.g., feelings, interests) and the world.

Keep in mind that strong, healthy, adult relationships are a two-way street. Just as you must experience others as nearby, a safe haven, and a secure base, it is important that they feel the same way about you. By reading this chapter and developing insights and skills related to relationships, your model of others will become more reliably available. Also, you will notice how this model of others and the model of self that you have been working on throughout this book feed each other. They will make you feel emotionally stronger and able to manage stress better. In the end, you will enjoy secure relationships without the high levels of sensitivity to rejection that have overwhelmed you in the past.

PROXIMITY: KEEPING LOVED ONES CLOSE

It is obvious that during early childhood, caregivers need to be near their children to keep them physically safe and to comfort them when they are distressed. What is less obvious is how essential this nearness—or what attachment theory calls *proximity*—is to helping people learn to cope with their emotions at that time and for the rest of their lives.

When caregivers (most often moms) are responsive to their children's needs, their children are not just *kept* safe, but they also *feel* safe, and eventually develop a secure attachment. They learn that they can turn to their caregivers to be comforted, and they eventually learn to comfort themselves. They also receive the message that they are lovable—whether smiling or wailing. Over time, they develop an inner *working* model that significant people in their lives will be caring, comforting, and accepting of them. With this working model as a part of how they experience themselves and the world, they have less of a need for their caregiver to be physically close to them because they have "internalized" this person. As a result, they are better at calming themselves when their attachment figures are not nearby.

Not only do these securely attached people have a *model of others* that is emotionally available, but they also have a *model of self* that is lovable and worthy. When they face difficult circumstances, their distress tends not to overtake them. Instead, they tend to respond with thoughts and behaviors that help them cope effectively with the situation. However, when the stresses and strain of life feel like too much, they are able—and do—turn to trusted others for support and reassurance.

As someone who is sensitive to rejection, you may have an anxious style of attachment. This would include holding a model of others that is often not emotionally available because of your model of self that is unlovable, unworthy, or inadequate. These inner models are apparent in Chad's constant scanning for signs of rejection from Linda, his chronic sense that he was falling short, and his fervent efforts to make Linda respond positively to him. Similarly, instead of feeling unconditionally accepted and comforted, you may feel driven to earn support and acceptance, making you sensitive to rejection.

However, you may have a more dismissing style, trying to prevent rejection by avoiding emotionally close relationships and by being extremely self-reliant. Many people with this style of attachment aren't fully aware of feeling particularly lonely, though this might underlie a sense of restlessness or boredom. Though you may generally do well in life, it can also leave you at a loss when facing overwhelmingly emotional issues and with a niggling sense of inner discomfort, especially in quiet moments.

So, to develop resilience to rejection, it is essential that you nurture a model of others that is emotionally available, along with a sense of yourself that is worthy and lovable. To do this, you must experience emotionally supportive people as close to your heart. Even more important than having them in physical proximity is carrying with you a working model of others that views them as emotionally available to comfort and support you.

Both ways of experiencing others as available provide a foundation for being able to look to others as a safe haven and also as a secure base. When you experience them as both, you will cope better with all kinds of social difficulties, from minor rebuffs to major rejections. So, the following sections on developing a safe haven and a secure base will also guide you in experiencing others as being close.

FINDING A SAFE HAVEN IN YOUR RELATIONSHIPS

"Thank you," Chad whispered to Linda, who replied with a gentle kiss to his forehead as she got up to refill their wineglasses. After talking intensely for the last hour about some problems at work, he finally felt better. He was still going to have to return tomorrow to the high-wire act that was his job (complete with a snarling boss below), but Linda's caring attention and ability to really appreciate his dilemma comforted him. Finally, after years of feeling alone, his relationship with Linda offered a safety zone where he could feel understood, soothed, reassured, and supported.

Attachment theory explains that people are wired from birth to look to others for their emotional safety needs. When people are upset or feel vulnerable, their attachment system is usually activated, prompting them to look for a significant person to help them feel safe. That attachment figure becomes a *safe haven* for them, and the comfort offered infuses them with the inner strength needed to navigate difficult circumstances.

To experience someone as a safe haven, they must be *emotionally attuned* to you. Not only would you feel they were empathic, but they would also be responsive to your emotional needs. Both empathy and responsiveness are conveyed verbally, but more importantly, they are also expressed in a variety of nonverbal ways. For instance, when Linda listened to Chad's struggles, her attentive gaze and the soft tone of her voice showed that she empathized. Her calmness, even when Chad became highly distressed, showed that she did not just join him emotionally, but that she was responsive to his need for a supportive, comforting presence.

Like many anxiously attached people, Chad often felt extremely alone and chronically flawed or inadequate, leaving him with a sense that he must repeatedly earn acceptance and work to prevent an inevitable rejection. Even though he desperately looked to others for acceptance and reassurance, he did not fully believe it when it was offered. By contrast, those with a more avoidant style of attachment don't even register the possibility of others being there for them. As a result, they tend to be excessively self-reliant. So, with both insecure attachment styles, there is a sense of being alone and a resistance to using others as a safe haven.

You can reduce your fear or expectation of rejection—and thus open yourself to others as a safe haven—by learning to recognize when you can trust someone to be accepting and supportive. An important sign is that you feel understood and comforted when you are with them. This does not mean that you feel privileged that they would deign to be kind to you (because, in your mind, you don't really deserve it), but that they seem to actually empathize with you and help you feel better about the situation *and* about yourself.

Identify Safe Havens in Your Life

For a relationship to be a safe haven, you must recognize the other person as someone you could turn to for comfort when you are upset. Get out your journal (or a sheet of paper) to help you do this exercise.

Make a written list of significant people currently in your life.

Circle the name of each person who fits with this list of traits. These characteristics describe people who can function well as a safe haven:

- Is a good listener, so you feel understood

- Expresses a desire to be there for you when you struggle

- Responds to your distress with caring, reassurance, and support

- Effectively communicates their support and caring

- Just being in their presence feels comforting

The people whose names you have circled are likely to be people you can rely on to comfort you and help relieve your distress at difficult times. Consider using the information in this chapter to help you work on turning to them (or turning to them more) when you are upset and fully taking in the comfort that they offer.

Reflecting on Comforting Relationships

Even when you know that someone in your life has been reliably there for you, you may still brace yourself for rejection. One way to build your sense of being able to rely on that person when you are going through a difficult time is to reflect on situations when they have been accepting and comforting.

Open Yourself to Feeling Comforted

Think back on a situation when you were upset and someone close to you responded with caring. Then do the following:

Note any warmth and positive feelings you had. Open yourself to really experiencing the relief you felt.

If you feel unable to access or hold the positive feelings, you may find it helpful to return to the chapter 5 section "Identifying Levels of Emotion." It offers insight into people's emotional reactions to their emotions—such as recognizing how you might respond to a primary emotion of feeling comforted with a defensive response of anxiety or emotionally distancing yourself. After processing this information, return to trying the current exercise again.

Note any anxiety about possible rejection. Your fear of rejection may be elicited when you lower your defenses in reaction to the caring response.

Allow yourself to hold the warm and anxious feelings at the same time. You might find it helpful to hold out your hands, palms up. Look at one hand as you connect with the warmth. Then look at your other hand as you connect with the fear of rejection. Then choose to refocus on the hand "holding" the sense of warm connection.

Reflect on the conflicting feelings. Note that your anxiety has more to do with your chronic fear of rejection than with any sign that this person will reject you.

Return your attention to the feeling of being comforted. Look at the palm that is "holding" the sense of feeling soothed. Allow yourself to feel cared about and relieved. Choose to put aside any anxiety about rejection, labeling it as a feeling that does not belong in this situation.

This exercise can help you connect more strongly with feeling cared about and experiencing a sense of relief from that. With repetition, perhaps choosing different situations with the same person, you may find it increasingly easy to trust in that person as a safe haven.

After reflecting on situations when a person has already comforted you in times of distress, consider using the strategy below to help you approach that person (or someone else) with something that is currently upsetting you.

Encourage Your Feeling of Safety in Relationships

This exercise involves increasing your feeling of being comforted while talking with someone about a topic that bothers you.

Choose a person who has already shown that they can be supportive and caring. If you struggle with fearing rejection, remind yourself that this person has shown themselves to be sensitive to your feelings.

Share a distressing topic with the person you have chosen. Pick a topic that bothers you, but does not make you too vulnerable. (If you have previously completed this exercise and feel reassured about the person's responsiveness, you may want to choose to a more sensitive topic.)

Pay attention to their response. As best as you can, objectively observe how they respond to your distress. When you see them show caring, consciously note that it is safe to let down your defenses enough to take in their support.

Linger on any sense of feeling comforted. Many people who struggle with rejection only briefly note that they feel comforted, and then immediately dive back into their sense of feeling unsafe. Instead, choose to spend more time focusing on the support and warmth you feel from the other person. Note any easing of your distress. If you still feel somewhat anxious, you might mentally respond with, *Yes, I feel anxious, but I'm safe with this person, and I'm going to pay attention to feeling comforted.*

Ask for a hug, if appropriate. As you may instinctively know, physical affection can be very soothing. For this reason, a simple hug (or holding hands) can help tremendously when you are upset. If you find physical affection uncomfortable, skip this step for now.

The more you practice opening yourself emotionally to others who show that they care about you, the more that these interactions will "warm your heart" and soothe your distressed feelings.

In completing this exercise, you might have trouble staying with a sense of feeling cared about. With this difficulty in mind, try returning to the exercise "Sit with Your Emotions" in chapter 5, "Emotions." Afterward, you might want to come back to this exercise.

If you struggled with the hugging part of the exercise, you might want to review the "Comforting Touch in Your Relationships" section of chapter 6, "Actions." This might help you develop your ability to appreciate touch as a way to feel soothed.

If you found any comfort in the interaction in this exercise, you can enhance the benefits of a comforting interaction by reminiscing about it.

Each time you revisit the interaction, you will reinforce your experience of being comforted by this person—making them more likely to be someone you can turn to as a safe haven.

Think of it as entering the person's warm home. Every time you repeat the experience, you become more assured that it will feel warm and soothing. You will begin to take off whatever layers of clothing and protection you have wrapped yourself in. But your anxieties and fears will, at times, likely make you wary of relaxing, reminding you to prepare for "when" the person will toss you out into the cold, threatening world. As you continue to challenge this fearful reaction, it will become less real and less powerful. Eventually, you will trust in the person's warm home as a safe haven.

Working Collaboratively to Create a Safe Haven

One frequently important element in establishing a safe haven in relationships is *collaborative communication*, which involves each person responding to the other. Consider this scenario:

> With a plaintive voice, Janine complained to Lucy, "I told my mother on the phone yesterday that I was planning to get a pet ferret, and she said, 'Why would you want to do that?' You know, in the way that she does." Looking at Lucy's blank expression, she exclaimed, "Oh, you don't understand. And you agree with her!" To ease Janine's distress, Lucy clarified that while she didn't have anything against ferrets, she also didn't get the attraction. "I have heard that they really smell. Have you thought about that?" she asked. Again, Janine felt hurt. But as the conversation progressed, Lucy assured Janine that she was good with Janine getting a ferret if it would make her happy. She added, "If your mother really is against the ferret, that's her problem." While it was clear to Janine that Lucy still didn't appreciate why she would want a ferret, she felt reassured, supported, and comforted.

In this situation, Janine and Lucy worked together, through collaborative communication, to understand each other, clarifying their thoughts and feelings along the way. This led to Janine feeling that Lucy was not judging her and that Lucy was someone she could turn to for comfort when she was upset. (Incidentally, this is very difficult to do "remotely" via social media, one of the big problems with using that form of communication.)

When you are struggling emotionally, you can benefit a lot from being able to turn to someone you trust to help ease your pain. Often, just their general caring is enough to comfort you. However, at other times, you will need reassurance that they truly understand and can empathize. Although they might immediately get it, you cannot always rely on this. Collaborative communication facilitates greater understanding, enabling them to really get what's going on for you. Then you are more likely to accept and feel comforted by their expressions of compassion, making them a safe haven during difficult times.

Active Listening

An effective method for engaging in collaborative communication is *active listening*. As you might intuitively expect, it means listening consciously and actively.

Practice active listening by choosing to talk with someone who is generally supportive and a good communicator. Pick an interesting topic to talk about, but not something that is likely to make you feel too vulnerable. You can always increase the difficulty as you practice it more and gain more skill. You might want to tell the person you are practicing active listening and even invite them to practice the steps with you—but neither is necessary. Finally, pick a time when you are unlikely to be distracted. Then use these steps to guide your conversation.

Pay attention. It's easy to get distracted while talking with people, so do your best to pay attention. When you catch yourself being distracted, redirect your focus back to what is being said.

Really listen. As you attend to the other person, focus on wanting to truly understand. Try to see the world through the other person's eyes, including having empathy with how they feel—even if you don't agree or think they are overreacting.

Show you are listening. It is extremely helpful for people to see that you are listening as they speak. This usually involves communicating through actions, as discussed in the "Understanding Nonverbal Communication" section of chapter 6. You might nod or offer vocal sounds of acknowledgment (e.g., "uh-huh"). Your body position—such as leaning forward or turning your head away—can say a lot, as well as your facial expressions.

When someone is discussing a difficult experience, you want to let them know you empathize, but are not lost in it with them. For instance, your eyes might tear up, but you would not be sobbing. By having your own empathic but less overwhelmed reaction, you can be a safe haven as you comfort them.

Reflect your understanding. Either confirm that you understand, or offer an opportunity for the other person to correct your misunderstanding. On its simplest level, this means telling the other person what you heard. However, a rote repetition of what someone says has the emotional depth and understanding of a robot. So, nonverbal communication is essential in expressing that you really "get" what they are saying.

If the other person indicates that you misunderstood, ask them to explain themselves again. Listen carefully and then try again to reflect what you are hearing. Do this as many times as necessary until the other person feels understood.

Offer your response. Depending on the conversation, you might offer validation, problem solve, or share your own experience or perspective. However, be sure to respond in these ways only after the other person feels listened to and understood.

With active listening, you will likely feel accepted, supported, and open to being vulnerable with that person. It's this way of relating that opens the possibility of you turning to the person for comfort when you need it—though not everyone can be good at comforting you, no matter how good the communication is.

ENCOURAGING PERSONAL GROWTH WITH A SECURE BASE

In addition to relationships offering a safe haven when you feel upset, they can serve the important function of being a *secure base*. Attachment theory explains that healthy, significant relationships support people in exploring their interests and the world. They encourage you to grow and develop as a person, which enables you to feel good about yourself and to have a sense of well-being. In the terms of attachment theory, you are supported in having a model of self as being worthy and a model of others as being emotionally supportive.

When someone is a secure base for you, they express caring and support for the "real" you. You do not need to earn their acceptance by behaving in specific ways, holding certain opinions, or achieving particular goals. Instead, they encourage you to explore what matters to you. This includes standing by you when you make false starts or stumble.

Importantly, they continue to support you even when your interests or opinions conflict with theirs. Without wavering in their support of you as a person, they might express concern about your decisions when they believe those decisions are not in your best interests. However, if they believe you are engaging in self-destructive behavior (such as drug abuse), they might remove support for that behavior. Through it all, they unconditionally care about you.

When partners (romantic or platonic) have a healthy relationship, they each serve as a secure base for the other. This means that they not only offer support, but they also look to each other for support when distressed. Partners can be supportive of each other even when tension exists between them. In these situations, they both feel the other has their best interests at heart, even as they work through their differences.

Identify Secure Bases in Your life

For a relationship to be a secure base, you must recognize the other person as someone you could turn to for support in your life journey. Get out your journal (or a sheet of paper) to help you do this exercise.

Copy down the list of people you have identified as a safe haven. You created this list in the exercise earlier in this chapter called "Identify Safe Havens in Your Life." If you did not complete this exercise before, do it now.

Circle the name of each person who fits with this list of traits. These characteristics describe people who can function well as a secure base.

Shows an interest in what's important to you

- Wants you to be the best version of yourself

- Encourages you to explore your interests

- Is consistent in their support and encouragement
- Is supportive even when you differ in opinion or interests

Consider whether you look for support from each person whose name is circled. For those whom you reach out to for encouragement in exploring your interests and values, place a star next to their names. They function as a secure base in your life. The other names that are circled represent potential secure bases.

Once you identify actual or secure bases in your life, you can begin strengthening them.

In completing this exercise, you might intellectually recognize that someone could be a secure base, but you still have trouble trusting in them. That's a common struggle that is similar to the struggle you may have in turning to others as a safe haven. You might find it helpful to return to the exercise earlier in this chapter entitled "Encourage Your Feeling of Safety in Relationships." By developing your ability to feel comforted by people as a safe haven, you will likely also be better able to turn to others as a secure base.

Growing with the Support of Friends

Fearing rejection often makes people conservative in how they lead their lives. For instance, Janine was only too aware of this when she was hesitant to tell her mother that she was getting a ferret, and then to share that conversation with Lucy. Although the voice in her head kept telling her to get a cat or a dog (which she was sure people would approve of), she decided on the ferret. She knew they were playfully curious, which she loved! This was a conscious act of bravery—risking disapproval in an effort to do something that made her happy. Even though her mother's reaction and Lucy's initial reaction at first made her second-guess herself, she felt better when she talked it through with Lucy and ultimately felt Lucy's support.

As you connect with your "true" self through increased self-awareness, you will become increasingly aware of your interests, values, and feelings. You may discover interests that friends don't have, realize beliefs that friends don't hold, or make decisions that they would not make. So, even then—especially then—it is important that you have people in your life whom you can rely on to be supportive of you exploring the world on your own terms. To do this, you must:

Identify people who are secure bases in your life. Use the above exercise, "Identify Secure Bases in Your Life," to identify people who could be (or already are) supportive of your personal growth.

Open up to supportive people. When you decide someone is safe to trust, your fear might still be strong. You can begin to test out their trustworthiness and challenge your fear by taking small chances. Divulge an interest or opinion that you wouldn't ordinarily express, but that is not too personal. Repeatedly do this, increasing your openness as you feel ready to take more risks.

Identify areas of personal growth. Consider your interests, values, feelings, and desires. Make a decision to explore these areas and to be more open to your emotions related to them.

Use supportive people as secure bases while investing yourself in personal growth. Reach out to people you have identified as secure bases, or potential ones. Allow them to be supportive of your pursuits, share in your excitement and concerns, and help you follow through with your goals.

You can, of course, explore your values and new interests without the support of anyone. But stretching yourself in these ways requires inner strength that can be enhanced by others acting as secure bases. Also, this kind of connection to others offers a sense of meaning and fulfillment that is missing from a life that is lived emotionally—if not physically—alone.

Challenging Self-Criticism with a Secure Base

Despite Janine's initial excitement about opening a café art gallery, she struggled with feeling like she was too dumb to do it or to even take a class about starting her own business. It was only after a motivating conversation with Beth that she felt like she might have what it took to learn enough from the class to move toward her goal.

You may seriously question that others will support and encourage your personal growth not just because of your fear that they'll reject you, but also because of your negative self-perceptions. It's almost impossible to believe their encouragement when you constantly question and undermine it with your harsh judgments of yourself and your abilities. However, when you have people in your life who are fully there for you emotionally (as Beth was for Janine), you will benefit from learning to take in their support and encouragement.

As you look to achieve personal goals, it is important to encourage yourself, as well as to feel encouraged by others, who can function as a secure base. Their support can help you challenge your self-criticism, see yourself in a more positive light, and pursue your dreams.

Use a Secure Base to Help You Persist Toward Your Goal

If judging yourself harshly gets in the way of you pursuing a goal, follow these steps to challenge self-criticism with a secure base relationship:

Choose a trusted person to speak with about your goal. This person must be someone who has shown themselves to be encouraging and is someone you named by completing this chapter's exercise, "Identify Secure Bases in Your Life."

Acknowledge negativity toward yourself. By seeing when you are being self-critical, you are also recognizing that there might be a more positive way to view yourself. (If you have trouble being aware of self-critical thoughts, you can work on this by reviewing chapter 4, "Thoughts.")

Talk about your struggle with your chosen confidante. This person will hopefully help you feel comforted by truly listening, understanding, and empathizing with you. Let the person know what your goal is and how you feel about it and yourself.

Listen carefully to their response. As they respond, allow yourself to feel their support (assuming they are encouraging). Try seeing yourself through their eyes.

Repeat back what you are hearing. If they are encouraging and you can really see yourself as they do, talking about yourself from their perspective can help reinforce positive perceptions of yourself.

With the support and encouragement of someone who is truly a secure base, you will hopefully take this conversation to heart and feel more positively about yourself and your ability to pursue your goal. However, self-doubts may arise at any point. If they do, return to the person who is your confidante and secure base (or to memories of your conversations) as many times as necessary for encouragement as you continue to struggle and grow.

It's important to understand that you can feel discouraged or rejected even by conversations in secure base relationships. If this happens, remind yourself that this person is usually supportive and not someone who wants to hurt you. Then take the brave step of talking with them about what you heard them say and how you feel about that—perhaps using the "Active Listening" exercise earlier in this chapter. Maybe you misunderstood. Or maybe they were more focused on saving you from possible distress than on empathizing with your thoughts, feelings, and desires. Or maybe there was some other misunderstanding. But hopefully this conversation will help provide greater clarity, leaving you to again feel like they are in your corner. Still, if you question their perspective or feel judged and rejected, you might choose to speak with someone else.

Aspirations to grow always hold with them the possibility of failure. Through encouragement within yourself and from secure base relationships, you can find the strength to persevere. Whether you meet with success or failure, you will feel positively about yourself and less concerned with being judged or rejected.

Carrying Your Secure Base Within

When you have repeated interactions with people (past and present) who function as safe havens and secure bases, you carry an abstract sense of them within you as *mental representations*. In other words, you keep them in close proximity to you, even when they are physically far away. Having attachment figures close by in this way forms the basis of a working model of others as emotionally available. (As you may remember, proximity is discussed in more detail in the beginning of this chapter.) Research has supported the idea that you can "prime" or strengthen this working model of others by consciously and repeatedly accessing the comfort and encouragement of these mental representations (Mikulincer, Shaver, and Pereg 2003).

Prime Your Secure Base

While there are many ways to prime your working model of others, this exercise offers a way to do it by using your phone.

Choose someone who is a secure base. Pick someone you have identified in the exercise "Identify Secure Bases in Your Life" (earlier in this chapter).

Find a picture of this person on your phone. While it can be any picture, it might be more helpful to choose a picture depicting a positive experience you had together.

Save this picture in an easily accessible place on your phone. You might make it your wallpaper or save it in a favorites album. The idea is that it should be easy to find.

Set an alarm on your phone to look at this picture every day. While this exercise is based on research showing that secure base priming is helpful, there is no evidence of the best way to do it or the best frequency. I suggest that you look at this picture at least once or twice a day.

Every time the alarm goes off, "prime" your connection as a secure base. Look at the picture and do the following:

- Pause long enough to revisit a memory of them being caring, supportive, and encouraging.

- Repeat the following sentences (aloud, if possible), which reflect the three basic elements of secure attachment: proximity, safe haven, and secure base. Repeat them slowly and with a connection to what you are saying (or thinking):

  _____ genuinely cares about me and just being near them is comforting.

  If I am upset, I can ask for help and they will probably be there for me. This would help me feel relieved and better able to cope.

> I can rely on _____ to support and encourage me in activities that I want to pursue.

You might print out or save the sentences on your phone so that you always have them with you. If you really connect with them, they can help you feel closer to your chosen secure base. The more you repeat them, the more deeply they can sink into your being.

Applying all you have learned in this chapter about nurturing relationships will combine with your efforts to increase self-awareness in the domains of STEAM, build self-acceptance, and nurture self-compassion. Together, they will give you greater inner strength, making you feel even better about yourself and less worried about rejection. Although you will be able to comfort yourself more, you (like all people) will still find it helps to think of, and spend time with, significant others—or attachment figures—in your life.

Postscript

Breathe. Just breathe, Chad advised himself while he waited for Linda's response. She swallowed slowly as she gazed at the ring. Then she looked deep into his eyes, as a smile curled the corner of her mouth. "I thought you'd never ask. Of course, I will." With a huge smile, he exhaled—or more accurately, he spontaneously deflated, as if her answer punctured his body, releasing the four years worth of tension he had held inside while trying to get up the nerve to ask her the big question.

Not that long ago, Janine never could have imagined that this would be her life. It was the opening night for her café art gallery. As she looked around, she was amazed. *My friends are all here! With all my fears and tears…and falling apart. I can't believe they have stuck with me.* For the first time in her life, she felt confident in herself, secure in her friendships, and truly looking forward to waking up tomorrow.

Sensitivity to rejection is like living in a house of mirrors when your own reflection makes you anxious. Looking at other people, you see rejection staring back—or perhaps you see a look of criticism forecasting imminent rejection. And so you focus intently on accomplishing something (anything), or on proving yourself. You think that if you can be productive or needed, then you will feel valued and safe…but that feeling never lasts.

By reading *Bouncing Back from Rejection,* you have bravely taken on the challenge of overcoming your sensitivity to rejection. It's okay if you still feel anxious and afraid, because that's what happens when people face their inner demons. Choosing to continue in your efforts is what ultimately matters.

Even as you have worked your way through this book, you may have felt a natural pull to constantly scan the responses of other people, on alert to discover rejection. All too frequently, you may immediately feel rejected and dive headlong into painful emotions. Hopefully, you have followed this book's suggestions to redirect your efforts to increasing your compassionate self-awareness. Even with the progress you have made, there is probably still more work to do. That's to be expected. This is a process that takes time.

Recommit yourself to putting in the effort to further develop compassionate self-awareness: getting to know, accept, and have compassion for yourself. Improving this skill will help you get better at tolerating, managing, and responding to painful emotions in a healthier way. You can then feel more positively about yourself, even when you are faced with the possibility—or reality—of rejection.

With this growing inner strength, you will no longer feel like you are living in a scary house of mirrors. You will not fear rejection at every turn. Of course, the responses of other people still matter a lot. No one likes rejection. But if it happens, you know that you will survive and move on. The sense of yourself as worthy and lovable will open you to experiencing relationships in which you feel accepted for you, comforted when upset, and encouraged to explore yourself and the world.

Rather than thinking about your journey from rejection sensitivity to resilience as a trip with a defined end, it may be more helpful to think of it as an adventure. You have actively deepened your self-awareness with STEAM, practiced self-compassion, and explored ways of experiencing your relationships with other people as sources of strength. Your connections with yourself and with others are entwined, feeding each other, making both stronger. As you have become less encumbered by fears of rejection, your adventure has become more motivated by your growing strength, resilience, and sense of well-being. You are venturing forward in *living* life, freer to simply enjoy being you.

List of Emotions

(Becker-Phelps 2014)

This list can also be found at www.drbecker-phelps.com/home/bouncing
-back/ or http://www.newharbinger.com/44024. Some people find it helpful
to keep the list handy so that they can check it when they are confused or
emotionally overwhelmed. You can download it and carry it with you.

HAPPY

At ease	Energetic	Optimistic
Ecstatic	Inspired	Satisfied
Hopeful	Relaxed	Wonderful
Pleased	Vital	Content
Thankful	Cheerful	Glad
Blissful	Excited	Peaceful
Elated	Lighthearted	Serene
Humorous	Relieved	Delighted
Proud	Well-Being	Grateful
Tranquil	Comfortable	Playful
Calm	Exhilarated	Spirited

COMPETENT

Adept	Strong	Secure
Capable	Arrogant	Together
Independent	Confident	Cocky
Powerful	Inspired	Important
Self-Reliant	Savvy	Invulnerable
Adequate	Thoughtful	Self-Assured
Composed	Brave	Worthy
Indestructible	Courageous	
Privileged	Invincible	

VALUED

Accepted	Cherished	Favored
Belonging	Loved	Understood
Included	Revered	Appreciated
Respected	Wanted	Desired
Worshiped	Adored	Idolized
Admired	Desirable	Validated

LOVING

Affectionate	Adoring	Enchanted
Attracted	Desirous	Infatuated
Fond	Horny	Passionate
Longing	Lustful	
Yearning	Aroused	

CARING

Compassionate	Tender	Liking
Connected	Concerned	Warm
Forgiving	Empathic	

INTERESTED

Absorbed	Eager	Resolute
Challenged	Fervent	Ardent
Determined	Motivated	Dedicated
Fascinated	Anticipating	Enthusiastic
Intrigued	Curious	Intent
Addicted	Engrossed	
Committed	Focused	

VINDICATED

Absolved	Forgiven	Redeemed
Appeased		

UNHAPPY

Agonized	Disillusioned	Melancholy
Discontented	Jealous	Sad
Hurt	Pessimistic	Despondent
Negative	Suspicious	Grief-stricken
Stressed	Crushed	Miserable
Alone	Dissatisfied	Shameful
Discouraged	Lonely	Detached
Inadequate	Regretful	Guilty
Pained	Tortured	Moody
Stubborn	Dark	Somber
Anguished	Envious	Disappointed
Disheartened	Low	Heartbroken
Inferior	Remorseful	Needy
Pathetic	Withdrawn	Startled
Sullen	Depressed	
Blue	Gloomy	

INSECURE

Awkward	Lost	Unsure
Confused	Torn	Common
Indecisive	Unfocused	Foolish
Surprised	Bewildered	Silly
Uncomfortable	Embarrassed	Uneasy
Baffled	Puzzled	Worthless
Disoriented	Uncertain	

OVERWHELMED

Burdened	Thwarted	Obliterated
Despairing	Worn out	Useless
Hopeless	Confused	Defeated
Pressured	Disorganized	Helpless
Worn down	Obligated	Powerless
Compelled	Trapped	Weak
Devastated	Consumed	
Impotent	Exhausted	

UNLOVED

Abandoned	Deserted	Judged
Criticized	Ignored	Rejected
Hated	Oppressed	Victimized
Lonely	Unsupported	Betrayed
Singled out	Alone	Disparaged
Aching	Discarded	Labeled
Cut off	Insignificant	Repulsive
Humiliated	Overlooked	Chastised
Misunderstood	Used	Excluded
Unlovable	Belittled	Left out
Alienated	Disgraced	Shamed

FEARFUL

Afraid	Anxious	Cautious
Cowardly	Distrustful	Dreading
Frightened	Horrified	Nervous
Paranoid	Scared	Suspicious
Terrified	Vulnerable	Concerned
Alarmed	Apprehensive	Exposed
Defenseless	Doubtful	Panicked
Hesitant	Hysterical	Tense
Petrified	Shaky	
Timid	Worried	

ANGRY

Aggressive	Outraged	Livid
Defiant	Appalled	Resentful
Fuming	Disgusted	Contemptuous
Infuriated	Hostile	Frustrated
Offended	Irritated	Indignant
Annoyed	Repulsed	Mad
Disdainful	Bitter	Scornful
Furious	Enraged	
Irate	Incensed	

INDIFFERENT

Ambivalent	Apathetic	Bored
Complacent	Flat	Lackadaisical
Lazy	Lethargic	Numb
Passive	Unmotivated	

SURPRISED

Amazed	Astonished	Shocked

Bibliography

Allen, J., E. Bleiberg, and T. Haslam-Hopwood. 2003. "Mentalizing as a Compass for Treatment." *Bulletin of the Menninger Clinic* 67: 1–11.

Barnard, L., and J. Curry. 2011. "Self-Compassion: Conceptualizations, Correlates, and Interventions." *Review of General Psychology* 15: 289–303.

Bartholomew, K., and L. Horowitz. 1991. "Attachment Styles Among Young Adults: A Test of a Four-Category Model." *Journal of Personality and Social Psychology* 61: 226–244.

Bowlby, J. 1969. *Attachment and Loss.* New York: Basic Books.

Briñol, P., M. Gascó, R. Petty, and J. Horcajo. 2013. "Treating Thoughts as Material Objects Can Increase or Decrease Their Impact on Evaluation." *Psychological Science* 24: 41–47.

Ekman, P. 2003. *Recognizing Faces and Feelings to Improve Communication and Emotional Life.* New York: Henry Holt.

Ekman, P. Atlas of Emotions. http://atlasofemotions.org.

Fonagy, P., and M. Target. 1997. "Attachment and Reflective Function: Their Role in Self-Organization." *Development and Psychopathology* 9: 679–700.

Fraley, C., A. Vicary, C. Brumbaugh, and G. Roisman. 2011. "Patterns of Stability in Adult Attachment: An Empirical Test of Two Models of Continuity and Change." *Journal of Personality and Social Psychology* 101: 974–992.

Gilbert, P. 2009. "Introducing Compassion-Focused Therapy." *Advances in Psychiatric Treatment* 15: 199–208.

Greenberg, L. 2010. "Emotion-Focused Therapy: A Clinical Synthesis." *FOCUS: The Journal of Lifelong Learning in Psychiatry* 8: 32–42.

Griffin, D., and K. Bartholomew. 1994. "The Metaphysics of Measurement: The Case of Adult Attachment." *Advances in Personal Relationships* 5: 17–52.

Hazan, C., and P. Shaver. 1987. "Romantic Love Conceptualized as an Attachment Process." *Journal of Personality and Social Psychology* 52: 511–524.

Kabat-Zinn, J. 1994. *Wherever You Go, There You Are: Mindfulness Meditation in Everyday Life.* New York: Hyperion.

Kornfield, J. 2008. *The Wise Heart: A Guide to the Universal Teachings of Buddhist Psychology.* Read by Jack Kornfield. Newark, NJ: Audible.

McQueen, A., and W. M. Klein. 2006. "Experimental Manipulations of Self-Affirmation: A Systematic Review." *Self and Identity* 5: 289–354.

Mikulincer, M., and P. Shaver. 2007. *Attachment in Adulthood: Structure, Dynamics, and Change*. New York: Guilford Press.

Mikulincer, M., P. Shaver, and D. Pereg. 2003. "Attachment Theory and Affect Regulation: The Dynamics, Development, and Cognitive Consequences of Attachment-Related Strategies." *Motivation and Emotion* 27: 77–102.

Neff, K. 2011. *Self-Compassion: The Proven Power of Being Kind to Yourself*. New York: William Morrow.

Neff, K. D., and C. Germer. 2017. "Self-Compassion and Psychological Wellbeing." In *Oxford Handbook of Compassion Science*, edited by E. M. Seppälä, E. Simon-Thomas, S. L. Brown, M. C. Worline, C. D. Cameron, and J. R. Doty. Oxford, UK: Oxford University Press.

Neff, K. D., and P. McGehee. 2010. "Self-Compassion and Psychological Resilience Among Adolescents and Young Adults." *Self and Identity* 9: 225–240.

Reis, S., and B. F. S. Grenyer. 2002. "Pathways to Anaclitic and Introjective Depression." *Psychology and Psychotherapy: Theory, Research and Practice* 75: 445–459.

Rumi, J. 1997. *The Illuminated Rumi*. Translated by C. Barks. New York: Broadway Books.

Siegel, D. 2010. *Mindsight: The New Science of Personal Transformation*. New York: Bantam Books.

Sonkin, D. J. n.d. "Can Secure Base Priming Enhance the Effects of Psychotherapy?" Accessed December 17, 2018. Retrieved from http://www.danielsonkin.com/articles/sbp_psychotherapy.html.

Steele, C. M. 1988. "The Psychology of Self-Affirmation: Sustaining the Integrity of the Self." *Advances in Experimental Social Psychology* 21: 261–302.

Waters, H., and E. Waters. 2006. "The Attachment Working Models Concept: Among Other Things, We Build Script-like Representations of Secure Base Experiences." *Attachment & Human Development* 8: 185–197.

Wei, M., K. Y. H. Liao, T. Y. Ku, and P. A. Shaffer. 2011. "Attachment, Self-Compassion, Empathy, and Subjective Well-Being Among College Students and Community Adults." *Journal of Personality* 79: 191–221.

Leslie Becker-Phelps, PhD, is an internationally published author, speaker, and psychologist. She is a trusted expert on relationship issues that people have with themselves, as well as with others. She is author of *Insecure in Love*. She writes the blogs *Making Change* for www.psychology today.com, and *Relationships* for www.webmd.com; and is the relationship expert for WebMD's Relationships message board. In addition, she has created a library of short videos on her YouTube channel to offer people the opportunity to learn how to feel better about themselves and their lives. Becker-Phelps has a private practice in Basking Ridge, NJ; and is on the medical staff of Robert Wood Johnson University Hospital Somerset, where she previously served as clinical director of women's psychological services, and chief of psychology in the department of psychiatry. She lives with her husband and two sons in Basking Ridge. Find out more about her at www.drbecker-phelps.com.

Foreword writer **Ronald D. Siegel, PsyD**, is assistant clinical professor of psychology at Harvard Medical School. He is a longtime student of mindfulness meditation, and serves on the board of directors and faculty at the Institute for Meditation and Psychotherapy. He teaches internationally about the application of mindfulness practice in psychotherapy and other fields, and maintains a private clinical practice in Lincoln, MA.

MORE BOOKS *from*
NEW HARBINGER PUBLICATIONS

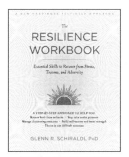

Register your **new harbinger** titles for additional benefits!

When you register your **new harbinger** title—purchased in any format, from any source—you get access to benefits like the following:

- Downloadable accessories like printable worksheets and extra content
- Instructional videos and audio files
- Information about updates, corrections, and new editions

Not every title has accessories, but we're adding new material all the time.

Access free accessories in 3 easy steps:

1. Sign in at NewHarbinger.com (or **register** to create an account).

2. Click on **register a book**. Search for your title and click the **register** button when it appears.

3. Click on the **book cover or title** to go to its details page. Click on **accessories** to view and access files.

That's all there is to it!

If you need help, visit:

NewHarbinger.com/accessories

new harbinger
CELEBRATING
40 YEARS